We Got Next

R. Deborah Davis, *Series Editor*

Rochelle Brock and Richard Greggory Johnson III
Executive Editors

Vol. 48

The Black Studies and Critical Thinking series
is part of the Peter Lang Education list.
Every volume is peer reviewed and meets
the highest quality standards for content and production.

PETER LANG
New York • Washington, D.C./Baltimore • Bern
Frankfurt • Berlin • Brussels • Vienna • Oxford

Lynnette Mawhinney

We Got Next

Urban Education and the Next Generation of Black Teachers

FOREWORD BY **H. Richard Milner IV**
AFTERWORD BY **Carol R. Rinke**

PETER LANG
New York • Washington, D.C./Baltimore • Bern
Frankfurt • Berlin • Brussels • Vienna • Oxford

Library of Congress Cataloging-in-Publication Data
Mawhinney, Lynnette.
We got next: urban education and the next generation of Black teachers /
Lynnette Mawhinney.
pages cm. — (Black studies and critical thinking; v. 48)
Includes bibliographical references.
1. Education, Urban—United States. 2. African American teachers.
3. Teachers—Training of—United States. I. Title.
LC5131.M36   370.9173'2—dc23   2013046485
ISBN 978-1-4331-2368-9 (hardcover)
ISBN 978-1-4331-2367-2 (paperback)
ISBN 978-1-4539-1281-2 (e-book)
ISSN 1947-5985

Bibliographic information published by **Die Deutsche Nationalbibliothek**.
Die Deutsche Nationalbibliothek lists this publication in the "Deutsche
Nationalbibliografie"; detailed bibliographic data is available
on the Internet at http://dnb.d-nb.de/.

© 2014 Peter Lang Publishing, Inc., New York
29 Broadway, 18th floor, New York, NY 10006
www.peterlang.com

All rights reserved.
Reprint or reproduction, even partially, in all forms such as microfilm,
xerography, microfiche, microcard, and offset strictly prohibited.

For all my past, present, and future students who share their lives with me and help me grow as a teacher. I am blessed to have you all in my life.

In memory of William and Jane Mawhinney.

CONTENTS

Acknowledgments	ix
Foreword	xi
Chapter 1. Introduction	1
Chapter 2. Carver University and Teacher Education	9
Chapter 3. Freshman Year: Thinking About Teaching	13
Chapter 4. Sophomore Year: Entering Teacher Education	49
Chapter 5. Junior Year: Practicing Teacher	87
Chapter 6. Senior Year: Certified Teacher	107
Chapter 7. We Got Next: Passing the Torch	119
Afterword: An Invitation to Dialogue About the Teaching Profession	123
Appendix: Interview Protocol	127
Notes	131
References	133

ACKNOWLEDGMENTS

This journey would not be possible without the support of Dr. Emery Petchauer and Dr. Kira Baker-Doyle. To Emery, I am eternally grateful to have you as a wonderful friend who pushes me to accomplish my best. Your support, loyalty, and honest critique have continued to humble me, and I am grateful to God to have you as a part of my life. To Kira, your wisdom and book coaching have been invaluable. You literally held my hand at the beginning of this process, and I appreciate your lovely support of my work and me.

Many thanks go to my homeboy, Dr. Decoteau Irby, and my homegirl, Dr. Laura Porterfield. You have both provided guidance, academically and spiritually, during this process, which was really needed at times. I am blessed to have two great friends like you both. Also, much love to my other writing group members, Dr. Sonia Rosen and Dr. Catriona MacLeod, for showing me the strength and beauty of mother-academics. A big shout-out goes to Dr. Tabitha Dell'Angelo, as I am honored each day to work, learn, and grow from you. I am privileged to have an amazing work partner and friend in a woman of great strength and a beautiful spirit like you. I also give a world of thanks to Dr. Carol Rinke, my writing partner and friend. It has been a great journey collaborating with you over the years, and I look forward to many more years working together. A huge Bahraini hug goes out to Jon Brown who was my greatest support and "hypeman" during the hardest and longest part of this book journey. I am so appreciative of all your gifts and what you have taught me thus far.

I am appreciative of TCNJ and the support they have provided to me to complete this book. Moreover, I am thankful for my colleagues, Dr. Alan Amtzis, Dr. Brenda Leake, Eileen Heddy, and Dr. Sarah Kern, for their continued support and push to make me a reflective teacher. I would also like to thank Dr. Rich Milner. Back at AERA in 2008, I heard you share valuable information about being a Black scholar, and every year since you have built on that knowledge for me. I am honored to have your support with the publication of this book.

On the home front, I would love to thank my parents, Katharine Mawhinney and Lawrence Mark, for instilling the importance of education in me and showing me the value of family. Thank you to my siblings, Bryan Coage, April Coage, and Nancy Rivera, and all my nieces and nephews. You have all made my life complete, and I love you dearly. Also, much love goes to my spiritual and surrogate sister, Lauren Egan, for all your love and prayers during this process. I could not do this without your continued support and faith in my abilities. Your passion for God, kindness toward others, and trust in people teaches me valuable lessons daily. A huge hug goes out to my best friend, Theresa Lane. Your courage, drive, and endless smiles are a treasure in my life. I am thankful to God that you are a part of my life and family.

My most important acknowledgment goes to the preservice teachers in this book (who will remain nameless) who have opened up their hearts and lives to me over these last couple of years. As your professor, and now your colleague, I have learned precious lessons from each of you. I thank you for all that you have shared and continue to teach me. Lastly, I would like to thank my Lord and Savior, Jesus Christ. I pray that I continue to do your will in this lifetime.

FOREWORD

Increasingly, I am asked to write forewords, epilogues, and back-cover blurbs for books in education, especially those focused on urban teaching, policy, and reform. In fact, I have had to decline such invitations for a few books for several reasons, including the following: the books were written from a deficit perspective about the communities and people they studied; the authors did not seem to deeply understand or articulate the real issues and challenges in the field; or the books did not make a significantly meaningful contribution to the field. Fortunately, this book, *We Got Next: Urban Education and the Next Generation of Black Teachers,* is the opposite. This book is written from the point of view of Black preservice teacher candidates and potential candidates. It showcases and speaks *to* and *through* their genius and potential while astutely highlighting organizational, structural, institutional, and systemic challenges that teacher candidates encounter on their journeys to become teachers. It is clear Mawhinney truly understands what can be conceptualized, studied, and practiced as two disparate fields—urban education and preservice teacher education, as she sheds light on the intersecting nature of them. Indeed, this is a serious book that will make an important contribution to what we know about the teacher education pipeline, urban education, as well as how to study the lived experiences of Black preservice teachers.

Drawing from a rich tradition of other Black teacher educators and researchers who have investigated some aspect of Black teachers, their identity, and teaching, such as Michelle Foster, Jackie Irvine, Gloria Ladson-Billings, and Vanessa Siddle-Walker, Mawhinney shifts the conversation regarding Black teachers away from what they do in the classroom to their preparation, triumphs and woes. Drawing from a life history framework, she "calls out" some of the under-examined and understated challenges Black prospective teachers face in their laborious journeys to become teachers, especially licensure examinations that attempt to measure candidates' basic skills. The discussion calls into question many unresolved issues: What is the relationship between teacher success/passage rates on these teacher examinations and their actual performances and practices in schools with students? What do these exams cover and what do they not examine in the grand narrative of what teachers need to know and be able to do in classrooms, especially in urban sociopolitical contexts? Why are these Black students underprepared to succeed on the examinations, and what roles have schools played in this lack of preparation? In what ways do these examinations serve as gatekeepers for potentially successful teachers in the field? And what can we learn from other fields such as social work, medicine, engineering, and nursing about what we as a field of teaching should and should *not* be doing given the particularistic nature of the profession of teaching?

Compellingly, this book updates the literature on Black teachers and their teaching by raising additional insights. For instance, what is covered in teacher education programs and why? Are Black teachers' experiences honored and addressed in these programs or are the programs tailored to meet the needs of White teachers mostly—given the current racial demography of teachers? What role can and should Historically Black Colleges and Universities play in the preparation of teachers, especially Black teachers at this time in history? And, perhaps most importantly, just where did the Black teaching force go (and why) after *Brown v. Board of Education*? In short, there is much to be learned from the stories of the 10 Black teachers represented in this volume.

There are perhaps no questions in education more important than those related to the racial demography of teachers in public schools—particularly for urban schools. Although the ethnic-matching research findings are scattered and inconclusive regarding the effects of Black teachers on Black student test scores, Black teachers bring into a classroom a set of expertise, insight, and experience that can never be fully measured. That is, Black teachers bring their lives and lived experiences into the classroom, and they become texts for their students: Their texts are filled with lessons from which Black (and other) students are able to learn and develop. Black teachers serve as role models for Black students. More times than not, they understand their Black students because they live similar experiences of racism and other forms of discrimination on a daily basis. Moreover, Black teachers often develop a form of fictive kinship with their Black students that bring out the best in their Black students.

Finally, it is no secret that students in urban communities—often students of color, those living below the poverty line, and those whose first language is not English—are grossly underserved in our educational system. Our obsession with test scores in the United States and the competitive U.S. nature have left many students feeling more like statistics than developing human beings with endless potential. In too many urban schools, students are stripped of many of the characteristics and qualities that make them complete and content: creativity, generosity, empathy, and curiosity. This book calls into question *who* teaches our children and encourages readers to recommit to increasing the Black teaching force in light of the reality that Black students continue to be an underserved group in public schools.

Indeed, during a time when the undervalue of Black children is at a premium, this book is right on time to help us all reimagine what Black teachers could do in service to all students in urban environments.

H. Richard Milner IV
University of Pittsburgh

· 1 ·

INTRODUCTION

Back in the late 1990s, I was one of two Black[1] preservice teachers in my class at a major Big Ten university with 40,000 students. It was evident then, as an African American, that I was part of a rare group of teachers. In all of my education courses, I remember looking around and not seeing a reflection of myself within my peers. Yet, this was often the norm throughout all of my educational experiences, and the experience of being the "token student" became normative quite quickly.

It was not until junior year that I had a class with another Black student. She was an older woman, in her mid-40s, named Brenda,[2] and we instantly gravitated to each other. In class, we partnered to create an adolescent literature teaching unit on American Indian life on reservations. While working together, we bonded over the concept of how important it was for us, as Black teachers, to be a role model for our future Black students. Sadly, Brenda, like many of the prospective Black teachers today, was unable to successfully pass the basic skills portion of the teacher certification exam. At our large university's graduation, I was the only Black face among the secondary education majors.

Brenda's struggle with teacher certification is not atypical in the education field. Since 2011, it has become increasingly harder for African Americans to enter the teaching field. For example, the "basic skills" portion of the teacher certification exams have become a roadblock for many Black preservice teachers to be admitted into a teacher education program (Bennett, McWhorter, & Kuykendall, 2006; Nettles, Scatton, Steinberg, & Tyler, 2011). Researchers have also cited issues of economic factors, academic performance and attainment, and social and cultural factors, which also impede the success rate of Black preservice teachers (Duhon-Sells, Peoples, Moore, & Page, 1996; Gordon, 2000).

This ultimately leaves a teaching field with a minimal Black teacher population. Only 6% of teachers are Black, as compared to their majority White counterparts, who make up 90% of the teaching population (Roberts & Irvine, 2009; U.S. Bureau of Labor Statistics, 2008). Even more shocking is that Black men only make up 1% of teachers (Lewis, 2006). This is a steep contrast to the large number of Black teachers who existed prior to the decision of *Brown v. Board of Education* to desegregate schools in the United States. So, quite simply, where did all the Black teachers go?

This book aims to tackle this question by exploring the lives of those few Black prospective teachers trying to enter the profession. The goal is to illustrate the many journeys that Black preservice teachers travel in their attempts to become teachers. It looks at their educational life histories—their schooling experiences, teaching philosophies, and personal motivations—to understand why they want to be teachers and the struggles and successes each of them encounters along the way. The book aims to push the discussion of diversity toward an alternative direction to fill a void in multicultural education literature.

Specifically, this book explores the educational life histories of 10 Black preservice teachers at a Historically Black University (HBCU). These pages give voice to their teaching motivations and perspectives on the profession through biography and personal narrative. It draws on earlier work suggesting that personal history and life experiences are vital in shaping classroom practice, professional relationships, and career direction. It investigates the unique struggles and successes of Black preservice teachers through their K–16 educational life histories.

Lives of Preservice Black Teachers

For decades, researchers and educators have struggled to understand how to develop a more diverse teaching force. Yet, interestingly, a majority of the research focuses on White teachers and their influences on students of color (Simmons, Lewis, & Larson, 2011; Sleeter, 2001). There are a few pieces of research, although quite limited, that capture the teacher stories of African Americans. Of the literature that exists, there are stories that revolve around the successes of extraordinary Black teachers in history (Etter-Lewis, 1996; Foster, 1996, 1997), Black teachers in urban contexts (Lewis, 2006; Lynn, 2002, 2006), and the lives of Black teachers in majority White schools (Kelly, 2007; Milner & Hoy, 2003).

However, there is the large missing component of the narratives of Black prospective teachers—preservice teachers. What are the expectations of these future Black teachers in the field of education? What successes and struggles do they have in their education programs? How do their K–12 educational experiences speak to how they see themselves as future teachers? More importantly, what motivates a Black college student to want to become a teacher? Boyer and Baptiste (1996) poignantly argue, "little research has been done on the personal experiences of those who apply to join the ranks of American educators" (p. 789).

Some life history studies started to address the lives and perspectives of underrepresented preservice teachers. Specifically, the studies look at how preservice teachers see themselves as future agents of change (Su, 1997), understanding notions of race in their future classrooms (Gomez & White, 2010), and their teacher education programs (Gomez, Rodriguez, & Agosto, 2008). These three research studies speak to the major needs of preservice teachers' lives and their connection to their future classrooms, yet only Su's (1997) study begins to address Black preservice teachers. Although teacher diversity is a major topic of study in universities and colleges of education, there are few texts that describe the experiences of Black teachers and even fewer about Black preservice teachers. Ultimately, as Su's (1997) research alludes to, Black preservice teachers' experiences are different, and it is time that Black future educators' stories enter the discussion through their own voices. It is through their voice that an alternative angle on diversity can push teacher education forward. Hence, the need to record their educational life histories becomes vitally important.

Life History as Theoretical Framework

Often, teacher education programs have preservice teachers reflect on their lives, experiences, and the connections made to their classrooms. This is because biography and personal narrative are intertwined within the pedagogical process (Carter & Doyle, 1996; Clandinin, 1986). Personal history and past educational and life experiences shape and mold teachers' classroom practices and professional relationships (Costigan, 2004). Rinke (2009) even discusses how life experiences can ultimately shape the career direction of teachers. Embracing this concept, the work reflected in this book is grounded in using life history as a methodological, as well as theoretical, framework.

Foster (1997) conducted work on Black novice and veteran teachers' life histories where she discusses the importance of life history work in connection with teachers:

> Life history not only provides material about individual lives but also offers the opportunity to explore how individual lives are shaped by society. Thus, life history research offers critical insights into larger social processes by connecting the lives to society (p. xxi).

Here, Foster suggests that the connection of teachers' past and future lives is linked to their understanding of society. Further, Goodson and Sikes (2001) frames three points of theoretical understanding concerning life histories in educational research. They explain:

1. It [life history method] explicitly recognizes that lives are not hermetically compartmentalized into, for example, the person we are at work (the professional self) and who we are at home (parent/child/partner selves), and that, consequently, anything which happens to us in one area of our lives potentially impacts upon and has implications for other areas too.
2. It acknowledges that there is a crucial interactive relationship between individuals' lives, their perceptions and experiences, and historical and social contexts and events.
3. It provides evidence to show how individuals negotiate their identities and, consequently, experience, create and make sense of the rules and roles of the social worlds in which they live. (p. 2)

The connection of life history as an active component to understand, complicate, and further define teachers' perspectives is the heart of this book. This is why this book explores the relationship of a life and the future teaching direction of preservice teachers with life history as a lens and driving force to the project.

Life History as Methodology

The life histories captured in this book are a small part to a larger research project called the Life Histories of Future Educators (LHFE) Project. The LHFE Project examined the educational life histories of 40 preservice teachers at three higher education institutions, one Historically Black University (HBCU) and two Predominantly White Institutions (PWIs), one a private, liberal arts undergraduate institution and the other a state university.

This book focuses on 10 of the 20 preservice teachers interviewed at the HBCU, all of which were my former students at the institution. The interviews and information presented took place over a seven-year period. A series of interviews were formally conducted and audiotaped to capture the Black preservice teachers' experiences. The purpose was to preserve the essence of their stories and voices, as their voices are the missing element to the discussion around teachers. The stories selected to be a part of this book were strong reflections of the whole group of participants.

Organization of the Book

In Chapter 2, I discuss the role and importance of HBCUs in preparing Black teachers and preservice teachers. Specifically, this chapter explores, in detail, the setting of this book, Carver University. The purpose of this chapter is to explain the intricacies of Carver University and its education program to provide a foreground for the preservice teachers' educational life histories.

The following chapters are segmented by four years: freshman, sophomore, junior, and senior years. Readers will meet prospective Black teachers from each of these years. In Chapter 3 (Freshman Year), readers will meet preservice teachers such as Allen, who came from a small, urban school district and moved around often as a child. When he finally met a mentor teacher and role model in high school, Allen started to seriously consider becoming a teacher. In Chapter 4 (Sophomore Year), Jessica will share her story of her passion for teaching, but also her struggle to successfully pass the basic skills portion of the teacher certification exam. This led Jessica to seek teacher certification in a neighboring state after graduation. Chapter 5 (Junior Year) highlights people such as Shironda. It was a struggle to reach college, but she fought her way in with a dream of becoming a teacher. Shironda had a stellar GPA in college and was the president of the Education Honors Society, and readers will see how her dreams of becoming a teacher were quickly shattered. Last, in

Chapter 6 (Senior Year), we hear the success story of Claresha and her quest to work within an Afrocentric school. She fulfilled this dream and has been teaching at an Afrocentric charter school for five years now.

Symbolism. Chapters 3 through 6 are symbolically organized to represent the declining number of Black prospective teachers. The Freshman Year starts off with four educational life histories representing how many come to major in education with great hopes, dreams, and intentions. By Sophomore Year, the number of Black prospective teachers starts to dwindle because of the educational roadblocks they experience. This smaller number is represented with only three educational life histories. By Junior Year and Senior Year, the number of Black preservice teachers entering the major drops significantly, as the preservice teachers face the harsh realities of the basic skills teacher certification exam. It is also at this point that the few Black men who come into the program sustain within the major. Thus, the Junior Year chapter is symbolized by only two voices. One was stuck in the cycle of "just one more try at the test," and the other successfully made it through the program. The symbolism ends with the Senior Year chapter, just one female voice, representing the small number of Black prospective teachers who actually make it to being a teacher.

Finally, the Conclusion chapter journeys back through the Black preservice teachers' stories. I widen the lens again concerning Black preservice teachers. Using the pieces of the preservice teachers' stories, I analyze the realities of their educational life histories and journey to becoming a teacher—whether successful or not. I draw on lessons from this study about obtaining and sustaining Black teachers in the field of education.

A Note on Format

The heart of this book focuses on the Black preservice teachers' experiences, struggles, and successes to becoming a teacher. These stories are written in the first-person voices and narratives of the preservice teachers. It is my goal in these chapters to preserve the authenticity of the preservice teachers' voices and experiences. There are moments, for fluidity of the reading, where the interview question is infused with the response.

For example, in Chapter 3, there is a segment when one of the preservice teachers, Allen, has the following exchange:

> **Question:** So you said you recently decided you wanted to be a teacher. How long ago was that do you think?
> **Allen:** The end of my 11th-grade year in high school.

In the chapter, this exchange is reflected as, "The end of my 11th-grade year in high school is when I decided to become a teacher." Moreover, some preservice teachers' narratives are also coupled with writings they created about their lives. Further there are moments where the participants might have spoken grammatically incorrect, for example, "I don't got no work," but the language was not changed to preserve the participants' voices.

At the end of each story, I step back from their voice to provide additional narratives to the preservice teachers' lives. I have built relationships with these preservice teachers as their professor, which I have sustained for more than seven years. Some of the narratives in their stories update their successes and struggles in the teacher education program past the initial life history interview. This added perspective comes from conversation over lunches or dinners, emails, Facebook, telephone, and events (i.e., graduations, wedding receptions, etc.).

· 2 ·
CARVER UNIVERSITY AND TEACHER EDUCATION

The stories that unfold within these pages highlight the educational life histories of preservice teachers attending a Historically Black University (HBCU). The Higher Education Act of 1965 defines an HBCU as the following:

> Any historically black college or university [hence, HBCU] that was established prior to 1964, whose principal mission was, and is, the education of black Americans, and that is accredited by a nationally recognized accrediting agency or association determined by the Secretary [of Education] to be a reliable authority as to the quality of training offered or is, according to such an agency or association, making reasonable progress toward accreditation (White House Initiative on Historically Black Colleges and Universities, 2013, p. 1).

Historically Black Colleges and Universities (HBCUs), like Carver University, have an important and unique role within teacher education. Many HBCUs were founded as normal schools (teacher training schools) before the turn of the century (Akbar & Sims, 2008; Irvine & Fenwick, 2011). The foundation of HBCUs as normal schools grew out of necessity as, before desegregation, African American schools were in need of African American teachers.

Even today, HBCUs still play a major role in diversifying the teaching field (Irvine & Fenwick, 2011). Although only 6% of the teaching population is Black (Roberts & Irvine, 2009; U.S. Bureau of Labor Statistics, 2008), 50% of Black public school teachers received their teaching certificate from an HBCU (Albritton, 2012). Moreover, the majority of HBCU teacher graduates opt to teach in high-needs areas (i.e., urban and rural districts) and consistently stay within these positions (Dilworth, 2012). As Dilworth (2012) explains, "the African American community and its colleges and universities have focused attention on the survival, maintenance, and advancement of their teacher education programs and the representation of African Americans in the teaching force" (p. 121).

Carver University tried to sustain a strong teacher education program but also struggled to maintain teacher education majors. This HBCU annually graduated the highest number of African American teachers in the state, which would range from 5 to 12 people each year. Carver's dedication to developing Black teachers was why the prospective teachers in this book were selected from this HBCU.

Carver University

Carver University is a small, rural HBCU situated on the East Coast of the United States. At the time of this study, Carver University had an enrollment of approximately 1,800 undergraduate students and 500 graduate students. There were 100 faculty members teaching at both the undergraduate and graduate campuses. The majority of the student population came from four majors cities spanning the East Coast (New York, Philadelphia, Baltimore, and Washington, DC). Most of the undergraduates were educated in public school systems within four cities.

Approximately half of Carver University students were the first people from their families to attend college. At the time, the average SAT score for Black Americans in the state was 810, and the average SAT score of incoming Carver University students was 850. On entering Carver University, students took a series of assessments on reading, math, and oral communication (speaking skills). For writing, they would determine if remediation was needed based on their SAT score. If students failed to meet the designated passing score, they were enrolled in remedial courses for the subject in need. There was one remedial course for writing, math, and oral communications, and there were two remedial courses for reading. These courses counted for credit and GPA, but they did not count for graduation. About two-thirds of Carver University students had to take at least one remedial course during their education, if not multiple courses. For some students, this prolonged their stay at Carver University beyond the traditional four-year window. The average six-year graduation rate was 44%, and the retention from freshman to sophomore year was about 70%.[3]

Teacher Education at Carver University

Interestingly, the Education Department at Carver University had two functions. First, three of the remedial courses (two reading and the oral communication courses) were housed in the department. The idea behind this decision was that many faculty in the department were K–12 teachers before entering the professoriate. Therefore, they could best assist with building the students' abilities.

The obvious second function of the department was for teacher education majors. At Carver University, students had the option to major in early childhood education, elementary education, and secondary education specializations in English, Social Studies, Mathematics, Foreign Languages, Health and Physical Education, and Biology. Special education was not an option at Carver University during this study.

According to the guidelines for teacher certification,[4] preservice teachers were not allowed to enter into their teaching major until they met three criteria: (1) a GPA of 3.0 or higher, (2) completed 30 credits of coursework, and (3) successfully passed all sections of the first (of two) teacher certification exams. The first part of the teacher certification exam consisted of three "basic skills" exams on reading, writing, and math. Historically, this teacher certification exam became a roadblock for many African American preservice teachers to even be admitted into a teacher education program (Bennett, McWhorter, & Kuykendall, 2006; Nettles, Scatton, Steinberg, & Tyler, 2011; Petchauer, 2012, 2013), and the education majors at Carver University were no different. For example, Nettles et al. (2011) found that less than half of African Americans pass the basic skills test on their first attempt compared to about 80% of their White counterparts. Moreover, the struggle and the pressure to pass this exam for Carver University students was more than just a grade. Petchauer (2013) highlights this aspect in this study about how one African American preservice teacher identified herself on the basic skills test as White in the hopes to successfully pass.

At Carver University, the majority of the preservice teachers had the GPA requirement and course requirements, but they were unable to successfully pass one or all sections of the basic skills teacher certification exam. During this study, some preservice teachers were able to be "grandfathered" in depending on when they entered Carver University. They were able to complete teacher education courses and graduate with a degree, but they were unable to work as a certified teacher. For other preservice teachers, dreams were shattered. Without the ability to pass the exam, or for some to maintain their GPA, they were counseled out into another major.

But often there was a vicious cycle that occurred at Carver University. Students would often just "hang in" for one more semester with the hopes of passing the basic skills exam to fulfill their dream of being a teacher. Each semester they would keep trying by taking the exam one more time, which also prolonged their degree and created more financial debt. The students would take random classes to stay enrolled in the hope of trying to take the exam to enter into the major. There were multiple times that the department had to council out fifth-year seniors because the "I'll-take-the-test-just-one-more-time" method to pass the basic skills exam was not successful. Students would finally relent and be counseled into a major of no interest (usually sociology) and graduate without any connection to teacher education. In short, the basic skills exam prevented many prospective Black teachers from entering the profession.

My Role at Carver University

I was a professor within the Department of Education at Carver University for three years. During that time, I taught two different developmental courses (oral communications and reading) along with teacher education courses in Educational Psychology and Urban Education. Before earning a PhD and entering higher education, I was an English teacher in Philadelphia. A number of my high school students went to Carver after graduation, and I joined them at Carver during their junior year at the university.

All the preservice teachers highlighted in this book were students in one of my teacher education courses. They were willing to open their lives concerning their K–12 educational experiences and also share their thoughts and feelings on their vision as a future teacher. Even past my duration at Carver University, I continue to have a professional relationship with most people in these pages.

· 3 ·
FRESHMAN YEAR:
THINKING ABOUT TEACHING

Allen

Allen took my remedial course in Critical Reading. The first day of class, most of my students were still navigating the transition between high school and college, but Allen was different. He sat in class, always attentive and pensive, but quiet with a chronic serious expression on his face. I quickly found out he was also a Secondary Education, Math major, and that Allen was attending the Education Club meetings on campus.

He had a caramel complexion with cornrows and green eyes. Many of the freshman girls in class would swing their attentions toward Allen, but his ability to hyper-focus on work made him miss all their flirtatious signals. Allen was a man on a mission, determined to succeed in college, as he was the first in his family from Newark, Delaware, to attend college. A month after the interview, Allen wrote a compelling and extremely honest autobiography in class, written in third person, and some of his writing is also shared below.

Home

I come from not a large family, but it was a nice size family, mother and father, two sisters and a brother. I'm the second oldest. I have an older sister by two years. She's not attending college yet, she's planning on attending a technical school in the spring semester. My little sister, she's 16, and my little brother is 14. My little sister is a freshman in high school, and my little brother is in the seventh grade.

I lived in Chester, Pennsylvania, until like the sixth grade, and then I moved to Claymont, Delaware. And then from there I moved to Newark. I can't really explain all the moving. Like all I know is while we was in Chester, we was moving from place to place cause of financial problems. And then we moved to Claymont, that's where we actually stayed for a while, and we had an efficiency. Then Mom and Dad wanted to have their own house, so they moved out of Claymont to a house in Newark. They don't own yet, but they're still working on it. Newark is not all urban. It depends on whether you live in the city of Newark or if you live on the outskirts of Newark—suburban. We live in townhouses on the outside of the city. *Allen further articulated in his third-person autobiographical piece:*

> Allen was born in Chester, PA, a city full of crime and drugs. Chester is a city with abandoned buildings, cracked sidewalks, homeless people, and dogs running loose; it is the perfect habitat for violence. As the city's population increased, so did the factors listed above. Can you imagine a young man like Allen walking to school at the age of nine, stepping over needles, condoms, broken bottles, and crack pipes? He witnessed this everyday because the school did not provide transportation, and his parents could not afford any either.

My mom is an assistant nurse, and my dad has been out of work for quite a while 'cause of disability. He had a couple jobs. He was a carver, like a meat cleaver at a factory, and he worked at a Pathmark, for more frequent jobs he had, and he got injured on the job. He got carpal tunnel, so he's been outta work for six years. He goes to therapy. He go like one time every two months for shots and stuff.

Both my mom and dad finished high school. I think my dad went into the military for a little bit, but I think he left. I think he was a medic, one of the people that remove the bodies. I don't know exactly what branch of military. But I know that's what he did when he was military and was removing the bodies. There was something else, but I don't get into too much of that. *Allen explained life at home in his autobiography:*

> The streets not only provided the image of drugs, sex and alcohol, but Allen was exposed to it at home as well. There was fighting among his parents and siblings. Drugs and alcohol abuse also took place in his house. He also spent a lot of time with his

older cousins, which created an alley to pornography and fornication. In Chester, he lived an unstable life. His family and he moved from placed to place, in and out of shelters, to living in one room at an aunt's house.

Allen's family finally found a sense of stability once they moved from their negative environment to the city of Claymont in Delaware. The neighborhood was a little better, but at this moment in his life, all he knew was drugs, sex, and alcohol and violence. Therefore, at the age of thirteen, Allen searched for what he knew. He searched for girls and drugs, but on the journey to find the drugs and girls, he developed a lust for money. Now instead of using drugs, he sold them.

K–12 Educational Experiences

I was in public schools all my life. I went to Sojourner Truth, I went there for kindergarten, and then I moved and I went to Tolkin from one through three, and then I moved back. So I was at Truth for fourth grade, and then I went to Simpson Middle in fifth grade, and that was before I moved to Delaware. And then I moved to Delaware. I went to Clariton Elementary for sixth grade, and then starting middle school for seventh and eighth, and then Christian High School from 9 through 12. The high school experience is the longest I've been at one school.

Truth and Tolkin, they're largely African American. In Delaware, it was a good mix, roughly half and half. I think Christian was more minority populated—it was more people of different races than White people in Christian. My class in high school was like a class of 240 something. But we had the biggest freshman class, and only 250 of us graduated. I think we started out with 600. *Allen explained the high school environment:*

> Just like Allen, his classmates were also exposed to sex, drugs and run down buildings, which the environment presented. Due to the environment, school was like a war zone. A day would not pass without several people being sent home for fighting. This was like an everyday process for him. It came to the point where teachers and administrators wondered, "Why do these students act the way they do? If they was taught manners and raised properly at home, than we would not have to put up with their behaviors."

Mostly the teachers talked until high school. And in high school, it was more interactive. I prefer more like hands-on learning. I like to do hands-on interaction. I think I retain the information better that way. So I guess I would say I'm a field dependent worker.

My GPA was a 3.4 in high school. I was an A/B student until I came to Delaware. I received my first C when I came to Delaware. But that was in

English, and I don't speak too well in English. *The first two years, behaviorally, were also a struggle for Allen in high school:*

> By now, Allen was enrolled into Christian High School as a freshman. Christian was not different than Chester; however, it did provide transportation. During his first two years at Christian, his sister and he drove the administration crazy. They were in the middle of physical confrontations before during and after school. Cursing teachers out, not being in the proper, and refusing to give their name when a faculty member asked for it was on there list. Overall they were defiant and were disruptions to not only their classes but also to the classes around them. So, if he was not in the office, than she was, they even went together sometimes.

I joined an organization called TSA, Technology Student Association, and that gave me some leadership skills and some networking skills on the job. I went two years to TSA. I found them very helpful. Problem solving, critical thinking, and so eventually using technology to solve a problem. So say as a group we had to build a bridge that holds 500 pounds and had to make that in class. So we would brainstorm, put them in design loop, and take our best idea and we would build a bridge. Then we would test it. After we tested it, if it didn't hold the 500, then we would rework it and retest it again. So eventually the design has no problems. Manufacturing and stuff like that.

At the state level, I participated in construction. One of our problems was we had to build a mini dollhouse, like a doll center, but you had to have a certain amount of grass, the dollhouse had to be no less than a certain height, and you had to have at least one side is shady. So me and my partner, which is my best friend, we did pretty good. They thought that we cheated 'cause in Delaware you can kind of—racists—I mean, not racist, but they didn't like the other side of the rubber. So we thought we had the best one there, but we got third place. And a teacher who judged our project phoned from our area, he said he gave us a perfect score.

As long as we participated at state, we can go to the national level. So we went to the national level, but you have to pass a test at the national before you can participate in that event. And there was a whole bunch of construction questions that we, me or my partner wasn't exposed to, so we didn't get a chance to participate, but we did take the test.

Another event that we participated in was structural—we had to build a bridge. We didn't do well in that. And my last year was in career comparison, where we had to research a career field. You had to research three different types of jobs within that field. You had to describe 'em, talk about their work, and stuff like that, and then you had to choose one. So you had to choose one, you had to come up with a cover letter and add a résumé, then you had to apply for the job. So I placed first place in speech on that one. But I didn't do too well at the national level. The first year of nationals was in Nashville, Tennessee, and the following year it was in Orlando, Florida. I was in National Honor Society at my high school, but other than that, there weren't any organizations I was in.

Mr. Epstein is my mentor. He was the advisor to the TSA organization. If it wasn't for him, I don't think I would be in college right now, 'cause he always told me, "Do your best. Don't settle for nothin' less than greatness," and he just pushed me. Like anything, I had a problem, school related or personal, I could go talk to him. I could call him right now and ask for his help for anything. We still talk once a week. I actually went to see him on Saturday, and on Friday, 'cause I go home every weekend and work. *Mr. Epstein was a big part of Allen's life:*

> During his junior year, he had a teacher that paid special attention to him. This teacher also became a male role model to Allen. The teachers' name was Mr. Epstein. Mr. Epstein got Allen involved in school ... Coming toward the end of the year, Allen received an invitation into the Honor Society. After Mr. Epstein talked him into doing it, Allen accepted this invitation and never looked back.

Church is not that big a part of my life, but I go when I can. Like most recently I been going to church with Mr. Epstein. I will go to church with him on Sundays, and his church is a little closer. My church is in Chester, so his is closer, so I will go with him to his church. But I haven't went since I came to Carver because I work Sunday mornings.

I hadn't had teachers as close as me and Epstein. I know teachers when I was younger, but I can't even remember as far as what they did to help me. But I know teachers helped me throughout my whole educational career, and I didn't have the support at home. Because they figure, 'cause I always made the grades, so everybody was, "Oh, yeah, Allen's gonna be fine. He knows what he's doin'. He's always gotten good grades," so like I ain't have the support at home, so I had a lot of support at school.

My last year at high school, my physics teacher. I didn't like the way he taught. And then when I would address a little problem or issue, he would just brush me off. He's like, "You don't know what you're talking about," or something like that. So he was like—that's probably the only bad experience I had with a teacher so far. But the crazy part is, no matter how much I got on his nerves, or he got on my nerves, I still passed with a D. I had him for 80 minutes, three times out of the week 'cause we had block scheduling. *Allen summed up his final year in high school:*

> All throughout his senior year, Allen stayed out of trouble. Of course, he had a few misunderstanding with some teachers, but they all resulted positively for him. His whole persona changed. He carried himself with respect and dignity. The administrators noticed his dramatic change and gave frequent complements. After a rough start, Allen finally got on the right path. With Mr. Epstein being on his back constantly and not allowing him to sell his self short; Allen became the first of his immediate family to go to college. Mr. Epstein also helped with the application and financial aid process.

Carver University

I'm the first in my immediate family to go to college. It made my parents realize that they didn't prepare well for our future, for their children, because the finances were never straight. I paid for college myself because my mom doesn't make enough to put me through college. And she's the one who pays all the bills. My dad gets a little check from disability, but that goes for his doctor's bills.

But other than that Boston Market pays pretty good. So I'm a manager there at the one back home in Delaware. I actually paid all my books. So all my books this semester out of pocket, and I just recently made a deposit, like today. So it pays pretty good. I get roughly like $400.00 every two weeks, just working weekends. So I just pay as I can for college. I have a car to get to Boston Market. Somebody come get me, somebody use my car to come get me.

It's like I was placed at Carver. I prayed about which school to go to, and I was told to stay home—close to home, and also, I didn't want to be in big classes, like a class of 150 students.

So I was originally accepted at a private college in Virginia. I was accepted there, but then I looked at the cost; I weighed it out. That was when I knew I would be gone, and so I finally got accepted by Carver, and I was like, "Yeah, that's closer to home. The class size is not that big, like 25 to a professor," so I was like, "Yeah, I can do Carver." And plus the cost again, so it was a couple thousand dollars less here, so I was like, "Yeah, I'll go to Carver." So I'm here.

My cousin on my dad's side of the family, he just recently got his master's from here. Then one of my members at the church graduated from here, so he talked highly about it. He talked about how they was loading their prestige back up.

Carver's not what I expected. I actually expected worse. I expected it to be big, more violent on campus, but it's okay. It's still people that act young and childish, but I stay to myself, so I don't find that as a big problem. It's just you have a lot of Black folks in one area. People tend to get arrested.

I'm in the Boys to Men Mentor program[5] and Education Club. I went to the Education Department's orientation meeting, and they went over the requirements before you can declare your major, so I'm actually trying to move towards that so I can declare as soon as possible.

Teaching Career

I recently wanted to be a teacher because teachers affected my life a lot. By the way, Mr. Epstein took me in and he matured me, and he developed me as a student and a person. I look forward to doing that same thing to somebody in a similar situation as me. So that's one of my nonfinancial goals is to at least bring in one person a year so that they can be professionals. In effect, I'll be a professional model for 'em.

The end of my 11th-grade year in high school is when I decided to become a teacher. Math, I thought, was a easy subject. I'm good with numbers, very good with numbers. So math, I pretty much went through my whole career with As and Bs in math. It just came naturally for me. Before that, I wanted to be a business major. I wanted to be an entrepreneur.

My family and friends, they didn't think much of me becoming a teacher. They just look at it as, "Yeah, you're going to college. Make the best of the situation." And that's pretty much it. They just wanted me to get the best out of my college experience and make sure I do my best.

My main goal as a teacher is the growth and maturing of young adults. The growth and maturing of 'em. That's my immediate goal. I'm wanting to build their skills, get 'em prepared for what the world is like, get 'em prepared for life and prepare 'em for the nationals at the same time. So I might get a lesson and I might do a activity with a part of the lesson to the real world, something like that.

My future classroom is going to be more hands-on, open discussion. We're going to work on our problem together, and then go back for homework and similar problems, similar to a college setting, but only introduce it to 'em at a younger age so that they'll be ready for college. Not as much as independent work, but more group work. It depends on my students' learning style, too. It'd depend on how the class is, how the students learn. I will observe that and then from there see how I'll teach each class. Some certain classes may not be able to handle group work 'cause they'll play and other classes will be able to handle it.

My relationships with my students will be about respect. You show respect; I give respect and vice versa. I won't come off as like a bad teacher, 'cause I want everybody to do well, but again in the same way, if you don't want yourself to do well, how can I push you to do well? You know what I mean? It's a certain level of respect you gotta have with your students. The same respect about you being a young Black male teaching. They're gonna be looking at me like, "Oh, you don't know what you're doing," because of my race and my age. 'Cause I get that a lot where I work at now. But other than that, it's the respect level, the respect all the way around. If you give respect, you get respect.

I want to teach somewhere in the tri-state area. So I mean Pennsylvania, Delaware, Jersey, somewhere in that area. I don't care if it's urban, suburban, or rural; whichever offers the most money. I'll teach in middle school, junior high.

Five years after graduation, I'll have a family, probably a kid or two. I'll probably go back to try to get my PhD, like in my spare time. But other than that, I just want to have a stable life. Yeah, I don't see no reason to jump around, unless I would lose my job, because I know in the Christian school district a lot of teachers lost their jobs because they [the school district] was in debt a couple million dollars. They was in debt a lot, so a lot of classes were cut, class sizes increased by almost 50%. So it was 32 kids in a class that only requires it to be 12. It was just crazy the last two years at Christian.

Ten years after graduation, I look forward to moving to a professor at a university. Probably be pretty well off, not too much unstable, but I'll be well off where as though, if a situation would arise, I would be able to handle the situation and still continue living a functional life. Again it's money, it's the connection with the world. I feel as though college students is the hope of the world right now, because that's our future doctors, lawyers, mathematicians, so interacting with the future world has been on my path because it allows me to understand what they're going through and allows me to connect with them.

Twenty years, I'll probably be looking forward to retire soon and stay home with my family. I plan on retiring like 45, 46. Yeah, I don't wanna retire late. I wanna have enough set aside for my retirement and for my child's education, my children's education, and not me doing some pretty tight budgeting.

****

A few weeks after this interview, Allen came to my office for advice. He wanted to blend both of his passions for business and education and change his major to business education. Unfortunately, Carver did not offer a business education major. We talked about the option of transferring to colleges that had business education or changing majors at Carver to business and going to graduate school for an education certificate. Allen opted for the second option, and he changed his major to business.

Once Allen changed his major, I saw him infrequently on campus, since his classes were held in buildings in a different part of campus. Two years later, I took another job at a different university. There would be an email here and there, but over time the communication dwindled.

The last time I saw Allen he was wearing his cap and gown and proudly graduating from Carver. I stopped him in the procession to give him a big hug of congratulations. He gave a slight smile, unusual for him. As he continued walking in the processional, I was reminded of his constant leaps over obstacles to become a college graduate. It made me reflect on his words freshman year:

> Allen was ideally one of the bad seeds that could not bear fruit; however after the proper guidance and just enough water, he spouted taller and brighter than his peers. There were other students around him that might have had better grades than him, but they were planted in the right soil. Allen emerged from unfertile soil that made him special. His father believed that Allen's life was a direct reflection of his; before he let the streets get the best of him. His mother always spoke highly of Allen and knew that he would amount to something more than a product of the streets. His older sister looked at Allen as her investment because she wished she could live the life that he did. His younger sister and brother looked at him as an inspiration. Allen did not allow his self to become a product of the street, because he knew that, one has the choice to break the cycle; it does not just magically break.

Leon

I first met Leon during the spring semester of his freshman year. He was a student in my evening Educational Psychology course and was majoring in Elementary Education. The course itself was in a room that traditionally sat 30 students, but due to overcrowding, the course now enrolled 40 students packed into a small space. Leon was always one of the first people to class and he would sit in the first seat, directly in front of me.

Although small in stature, Leon has a warm and charismatic nature. He had an intense stare when concentrating and his posture was almost as stiff as the small locks in his hair, but he also knew when to relax and have a good laugh in class. Born and raised in Pittsburgh, Leon relayed his story.

Home

I grew up on the outskirts of Pittsburgh, and it's pretty small. Some people just—they haven't even heard of it. I don't believe 'em [*laughter*]. It's me, my mother, and my little brother. I'm the oldest on my mother's side. And my little brother's 11 and we're all different. My little brother's, actually right now he's like the real active one. He's into all sports, anything like that. He's just real active—the average little boy. My sister, like she's 15 going on 30. My sister, she started off real good. She used to be with all her little friends, good grades, cheerleading. She did her little thing. Now she's just bad. You woulda thought that she was raised in some other place. She's bad. She like fights. She's loud, dramatic, all of the above, and I would say—but I think we all have a temper, but I think my sister can't control hers. My brother's just more like gets mad and be quiet. I think I can control mine. I think I'm more the calmer one outta the three. We're all different. My dad is in Pittsburgh as well.

My mom works at a bank. She's like a rep. I would say we were a middle-class family—like average. My mom, three kids. She's with some guy now I call my stepdad. He's been around five years, but he lives in DC to work back and forth so I don't know how it's going with that, but I would say about average. My mom graduated high school for her diploma, but I don't know if she finished college or not. I think she's going to school on the side of other stuff. I don't really know too much details about it.

After high school graduation, I moved to New York with my uncle. Actually, he's really my cousin, but since he's older, I call him my uncle. That's how that works. I used to always go up there (New York) with him 'cause he runs the YMCA camp. My first year I was older. I think I was 15 or 16, and I volunteered the whole summer as a counselor. Then the next year that's when I got to work for him as a counselor, and I've been doing that for three or four years now.

K–12 Educational Experiences

I went to the Common School District. I would put it like this. I wouldn't send my child to that school. I don't think it's a good district. It's like they're trying to make the school what it's not. They might try to make it look private or whatever you wanna call it—try to make us wear uniforms, painting up the place or whatever. I don't think it's a good school district.

It isn't bad, but I don't think people will learn nothing there really. I don't think these people cared for a lotta stuff. You had to learn yourself on a lotta things. My little brother, my mom just sent him to a school with his dad in the city. If he was going to a school in Common, he might have your average C grades now in his school now. Now that he goes to another school, he's on the honor roll there. He's doing real good there and he's learning stuff there he should've been learning. You don't learn what you should at the right rate compared to other schools. In fact, they're like two steps behind.

My school building is K through 12 in the same building. I don't think that's good neither because—it's not really a problem but for some people it's not good 'cause most kids, elementary, middle school, and high school are all different buildings and all different kids. I think that's good because when they go to college they'll be prepared to go to another school seeing as all of us that go to that school, we've been in that same school our whole life. So moving somewhere else is like a big transition going to their new school the first time, and it was when you go to your school for the first time, so I don't think that's really good. We had like 45 or less students that I graduated with. It was literally everybody knew your name. Out of 10 students, I would say seven and a half was Black and the rest two and a half was White. It's a good balance, I think. If there was like 10 teachers in our school, maybe three of them are Black—four maybe.

My favorite teacher—third grade, Ms. Williams. She was just a big teacher. She'd work with you. She was always just happy. Then her free time was to give you a snack. We would have to work for it as a class and at the end of the day she'd always be waiting for her little stories, and the thing that's so crazy, she might teach at that school for years, but like I said, you had her as a teacher she was telling that same story to each student but just messing up the name. We used to tell the older students. She's be like, "We had that story too, but she'd mix it up, but it was basically the same." We'd all be amazed how she remembers it, but she used to do that for us all the time. I thought she was a good teacher.

I don't think I have one favorite teacher for middle school. They were all pretty much drawlin'[6] to me. My favorite high school teacher was—they had a few I liked. I liked the workshop teacher 'cause I used to wanna be an architect, but I think that's more of a hobby. I don't think I want to work outside in the cold or nothing where I can't feel my hands or something. I liked the workshop teacher. My English teacher. She was pretty good. She was always happy. So was my other English teacher, Mr. McCarthy 'cause when you walked in his room I guess it was by the windows. It was real peaceful—real nice and cool, and he was mellow when he teached, so it was pretty good. Oh, Mr. Beeker my math teacher; I liked him and how he taught. I had a B in his class. He explains it so you can understand it. He taught pretty well, and then in some of my classes I was like—what do they call it? Special ed now, like resource? All the teachers were Black, like Ms. Jones. I still talk to her sometimes.

My IEP came when I was in elementary. I don't know. I am not really sure how it came about. I'm not sure. I could not read. I don't know if I couldn't read or I just didn't have the patience for it 'cause I still don't have a good patience for it. I lose attention on it real fast. I fall asleep or something. Maybe it was then when—yeah, I think might have been late elementary, like around fourth grade.

In middle school, Mr. Brennan was my least favorite teacher. He would just walk into his room and be ready to leave as soon as you get there because he—I don't know if he don't like kids or just people or something. He just comes off like that—just mean—and he just comes off like, "Wow." Like I wouldn't invite him to dinner. We'd be the only class in there reading a history book or something. I'm not saying that he wouldn't treat us and stuff, but he was just uptight. I always said his underwear was too tight or something. He's still there now.

The worst teacher is the high school math teacher who ended up turning into the track coach back then, what's her name, and I usually like young teachers because they be more bright. They be more up to date and everything through their music, like I would still be young and they still go out, and she was just the total opposite. She might be the youngest teacher I ever had. She was under 26 maybe, and she'd come in there, come into the math class like it was art, and it was a small class. It had to be five of us in that class. Everybody should've been passing and which we were not. She was rude, smart mouthed. I remember I had got into it with her one day because she doesn't want anybody to chew gum in her room. Understandable I guess, but she's chewing gum, so I had runned my mouth and she made me spit it out, or I'll have like this type of detention or something, and I was like, "But you're chewing gum just like I am. You talk to us more than we talk to you, so maybe that gum with stop you from talking, right." She was mad. I got a detention.

She didn't get a good point. I ended up dropping her class to go to the resource room 'cause I refused to go to that room because I knew I would have failed it. I didn't like the teacher at all, so it just would never had worked.

Carver University

Honestly? At the time I was like—I seen that new movie *Stomp the Yard*, so I wanted to go somewhere where it looked just like that campus, and I had my mom search everywhere looking for a campus that looked something like that, so that was my goal, and which I didn't find it. We had found a school in Florida. We knew it was like Florida A&M or something A&M.

We wasn't sure, but I had got accepted to an HBCU in Florida, and then my best friend was gonna go to the same school, but I don't know what we did. We switched, and then I was gonna go to Virginia. That's where—that was my first choice. Me and my best friend were going to the same school.

That was our first choice, but I had got accepted for the spring semester and she did not, so we didn't go to that, and then we visited Carver. I had came to Carver on a Wednesday 'cause I know somebody that goes here. Everybody was outside, it was hot, but I thought, "Oh, it's like the movies," so I said, "I think I wanna come here," and the other choice was Virginia. At the time, I wanted to go to Virginia as well, but I had visited the school and I hated the campus. It looked dirty to me, so I said, "Okay. Carver's my next best choice," so I went to Carver.

My best friend went to school in Erie for sports. She plays basketball so we had to end up going that way. I might transfer maybe in a few years to go to the same school with her. I didn't go to Virginia 'cause she didn't get accepted to it and I didn't wanna go to such a big school by myself. I was like, I could put that on hold and wait.

As we speak, my family don't want me to be here, especially my mom. She's like, "I don't know why you're going to that ghetto school. They don't do nothing right," and which they don't sometimes, so I can't be mad at her for that, and she still tries to influence me to transfer now. Even when I talk to her, "I'll help you apply somewhere else." She said I shoulda went to Virginia, or she said I should try to go to an HBCU down south or something, or try some school in Atlanta or somewhere. She just don't want me to be at Carver. She thinks it's a dumb school.

It's not the education. I think it's more like the system, 'cause they do a lotta stuff that's ridiculous. When I first came to this school first semester, everybody was hyped up with their roommate, and I hadn't met my roommate. He's from New York so I hadn't met him. I was going on meet him. My mom took me to meet him, and we got to this school and everything was all right, but he didn't have none of his supplies or nothing, so I was like, "We can share. We're roommates. We'll have to work together."

So everything was going good the first couple weeks and then he started smoking weed in the room. I didn't really care, but then it started getting too much. It was midterm week, and I was going to sleep at 2:00 a.m.

Some of his friends come in. They were loud, so we get into it and then I got him kicked out the room, so he was mad. We got into talking, and he had took my glasses out my room—stole 'em. And I was like, "I ain't gonna leave my stuff in here for him to steal it again," so I had to move all my stuff out the room and put it into the next dorm. I just removed my stuff out the room, so I didn't have no room for two weeks like I had to stay with my friends and was on the floor, and of course my mom was mad about that because she was like, "You should'na been the one leaving. It shoulda been him," so she was calling up the school cussing them out waiting for me to get a room, 'cause then they sent me into the guest quarters for a week.

That was fine, but I had to move again, so then they had moved me back to the room after that week 'cause he had got kicked outta school. He got caught smoking weed. He got kicked out, but when I went back into the room all his junk was just everywhere in the room 'cause I guess the police was going through it and they just left it a mess, but my mom was like, "How they gonna send you back to that room with the room looking like that with his stuff everywhere? It shoulda been emptied out," so she was mad about that.

That was their first mistake, and then she was mad about they had charged me over credit. I think I had 16 credits. They was charging me for 19 or something, so I had looked on it and I'm like, They're overcharging me. She was mad about that.

Then something happened with me financially, she was mad about. With this school, if you received a scholarship you have to finish it first or you can't finish your financial aid or something. At the time, they want you to send it to financial aid, not bursar, and my scholarship sent it to the bursar's office thinking it was just Carver, it's all a system, as I would think too but it wasn't, so then they gave me a refund for almost $2,000.00—so they had gave me that big refund and I ended up owing $1,000.00-some, and then my mom thinks, "Why would you give me back so much money if I owed you that much?" and I also kept it. And then because the check came to the wrong place and, "We didn't know you were receiving it." It was a long story with that, so I had to pay them back. The scholarship is O.V.R. I got it in high school. It said as long as I keep a GPA of a 2.5 and up, I receive $2,000.00 every semester.

I heard Carver had a great education program. That's all I heard. I hadn't heard too much else besides that. Filling out applications and going to colleges is more my best friend helping me. I was real lazy at it, but a lotta people applied for schools in October and December. I didn't decide to apply to school till January. I was real late, and she was getting on me about it.

My mom, my aunt, and my grandma got on me about it, finding me all the things I need for school. My mom thought that was the financial aid. I filled out the FAFSA and stuff, but making me apply, that was my best friend.

Teaching Career

I don't wanna work with any kids between fifth grade and 12th 'cause that's when they have an attitude where they think they already know too much, and I have good patience with kids, but I don't know if they were mouthing me off I could sit there, so little kids is fun. They're easy to work with and I have background working with kids that age, so I like working with them and helping them. Maybe that's why I picked elementary.

My uncle's wife is a teacher. I think she teaches fourth or fifth grade. I think she teaches fourth or fifth grade, and I was talking to her about it, and somewhere with that I wanted to get a performing arts school for kids and maybe be a principal for that or run it, and I may have to start with education to do it. So I'd rather start off with elementary with something I'm more comfortable with and something I think I'd like to do if I'm doing it.

I think I would be good at running a school—if it was a performing arts school place thing, I think I'd be good at that. I think I'm good at making up ideas to situations like that. I really think I would, 'cause I would work well doing something like that. I don't know if I would not pick a performing arts school. I think it might be boring. I think it might be boring if it wasn't. My idea of how principals work now, it's more authority, less involved. The reason I want to be a principal in a performing arts school, I feel like I'd be able to be involved in the active activities or have a option and input. The principal's like a regular teacher. They don't do nothing. I think the teachers have more power than the principal in a regular school 'cause he don't say nothing but yes or no. I don't even know the choices on that degree to become a principal.

Well, of course my uncle's this outdoors teacher. My mom—I'm trying to think of a quote. I can see her face when she says it. Like, "You wanna be that?! Nothing wrong with being a teacher, but I think you should be looking for something else because you won't get too much money in it. I mean, I wanna eat." She said something like that. My aunt, she's more accepting with it though. "Well, Leon, it's whatever you like." My grandma, I guess she's more accepting with it, too. But she can be like me mom too. Like, "Well, Leon, what you wanna do?," and tell jokes with a smile.

At first, I wanted to be a psychologist for kids. My grandma was like, "Ohhh, so why work with some kids." It really wouldn't matter what age, but she was like, "Be careful." Some kids could say you touched them the wrong way and I really don't wanna deal with that hassle.

My mom was like, "Why don't you go back into the psychology thing? What happened with you wanting to do that?" Now you gonna think, what's gonna support you or whatever else. That's what she pretty much said.

After graduation, I'd like to teach, I think maybe first grade, a kindergarten class, maybe second. I have to give more thought on it. Five years after graduation, I know what I want to do, which is everything I need to know to get to what I wanna do, like a principal of a performing arts school and everything.

I think I would definitely enjoy it being a principal. I want to have a job that I want to wake up and want to go to work. I don't wanna wake up and be like, "I hate my life. I hate my job." I think that's the worst thing ever, to have a job that you're not happy doing. But I think I would be satisfied with that. I also gotta know enough things career wise—stuff to fall back on 'cause I don't wanna choose the wrong thing and not be happy doing it. Go far in something and then have it not work.

Basic Skills Certification Exam

With the basic skills exam, I'm not big on tests, especially timed tests 'cause you be rushing, and my brain don't think fast enough to see everything. That's probably why I'm in the Critical Reading[7] and with that reading tests and you gotta answer all the questions. When I read it takes me a minute to comprehend all that, and honestly when I saw that test I don't know if I'll take it again for the region at a price mainly. It's just a high price for a test like that to fail, so I don't know. I couldn't handle that. I hope I don't fail it.

I understand the concept of the basic skills exam. I agree with the concept. I think if it was free or something, I would probably take it as many times as I had to. I don't like paying for something like that. I don't like wasting money. It's not wasting money, but if you just flunked a test that just cost $170.00, it's like, "Wow." You might as well just thrown it out the window.

I definitely think the test will stop me from being an education major. I get discouraged real fast on some things, and I was getting discouraged when we was applying for it.[8] I planned just to walk out the room, but I didn't wanna just walk out the room while everybody's just sitting there watching me, but I don't know, but it was discouraging me at one point. If I did stop, I might just find a career. I know, like a decent one. I don't wanna do accounting. I'm not fond of math. What would I do? I'd still wanna work with kids somehow. I'd just work in performing arts somehow—either or. I know I'd be happy doing it. Other than that, I'm not sure.

****

The years following freshman year, Leon's locks became longer and his positive energy more contagious. Opposite of his mother's initial wishes, Leon did stay at Carver University for the duration of his college career. He gained the prestigious role of being the head ambassador of the university and president of an elite club on campus. Leon also became a member of a well-known Black fraternity, and he was an intricate part of the campus life up to his graduation in 2012.

Leon was right in his prediction freshman year. He did sign up to take the basic skills exam, but he missed the bus that morning to the testing site. He signed up for the exam again, but he did not meet the state's passing requirements. He decided to take the exam only once. Due to the exam, and other issues within the Education Department, Leon made the decision to switch majors. Around junior year, Leon changed majors to sociology. The degree allowed him to tailor his sociology degree to have an emphasis in education, and he minored in human services. Leon articulated his decision to switch majors in an email five years later:

> It was the [basic skills exam] that made me switch majors and also the fact that a lot of unfair things were happening within the Education department. I also, at the time, did not plan to teach in [the state] and was under the impression that [the exam] only certified for you [this state]. And do I regret it, yes and no … yes, because the Soc. department is no better and I feel a lot of the teachers taught close minded with no real passion for their students to learn, No because it may have been a lose-lose. Either way I didn't want to risk being one of those students held back in the education department for rules that everyone did not follow in order to graduate that may have caused me to stay too long.

Since Carver University, Leon has been actively pursuing graduate schools to study interior architecture. He still hopes to pursue his dreams of dance and being involved in the performance arts. Leon articulated his thoughts on leaving the teaching profession:

> I am putting education to the side because I am not going to be young forever, and education is not going anywhere. But to me, the ability to do some things while you are young is not as endless like education.

Tierra

Tierra was a lively, spunky track star at Carver University. She stood at about 5'1" tall, but she was built like a rock. Tierra was always in workout gear and running into the room just as class would start, as she was coming directly from track practice. A friend of Leon's, as they were both Elementary Education majors, Tierra would always sit next to Leon in the front row—just in time for the lesson to begin.

With flawless skin and a radiant smile, Tierra had a striking natural beauty, and it was hard to imagine that there are two of her, as she had an identical twin sister at another nearby university. A Baltimore native, Tierra recounted her story.

Home

I grew up in Baltimore City. I actually grew up in the ghetto projects. We actually grew up hard until I got to the fourth grade. That's when my mom—we had to move into a house. We always lived in townhomes or—my whole family, we always lived in one house and had one little house. We always made it 'cause rent was always cheaper with everybody living together, but I grew up in hard Baltimore City where all the trouble is—the bad part of Baltimore City.

I have three siblings. I have three on my mother's side and one on my father. I don't really know him, though. My brother was first, and then it's me and then it's my sister. We were a minute after each other. My brother's actually two years older than us.

My mom passed away when we were 11. She got in a car accident December of 2000 from a drunk driver. They put a metal rod in her leg, her femur, and they didn't know she had blood clots in her legs from the metal, and she was taking some medicine called Prednisone that gave her heart poisoning as well.

So combined together, she had five heart attacks, and then she finally passed away. After my mom passed away, me and my sister lived with my aunt and my brother lived with my uncle, and my sister got in an altercation, so my sister moved with my grandmother, and then my grandmother passed away. My sister moved with my cousin. Now she's kinda living with my cousin. My aunt was in the good part of Baltimore. Well, not when I was little, 'cause she was the first one to move out the city. She lived in—she was in Baltimore County—the good part, so she lived in a good neighborhood.

My brother's actually gonna move with my cousin 'cause he's not in school. He was at a Historically Black University in the South, but not anymore 'cause the whole thing with him being incarcerated and everything. He was in the end of his freshman year when he got incarcerated. It was a guy that we knew for about 10 years up here named Joshy. Joshy actually went to Carver University last year. He was having family problems. He and his mom couldn't pay for rent at their house, and so he was even robbing stores up here and he got expelled, but nobody knew that was with my brother, so he went home and asked my brother to help him get money for the house. So they both robbed stores, and when Joshy got caught my brother didn't. They didn't really catch my brother at first.

It actually died down two months, and the cops went to my uncle's house with a state warrant. They thought he actually used to live there. Instead he'd been there hopping, and my uncle called my brother and said he had to turn himself in 'cause of what happened to his house, so my brother turned himself in and he had 18 months, but he's only been there for a year and he gets out Sunday. When he get out, he's gonna try to get back on his feet and go back to school. My cousin said she was gonna let him stay with her. He has to pay half the rent and everything. She's gonna help him get back on his feet.

My cousin's gonna pick me up so we can go back home, 'cause my brother didn't see me graduate and he didn't see me off to prom. This isn't his first time he's been incarcerated. It was the same thing. It's actually pretty funny 'cause last time when I was a junior he missed my prom 'cause of the same situation he was incarcerated for the same situation, but he seen my sister's prom, and when he went in, it was like, "You gonna miss my prom again?! You miss my prom twice. Man you have problems" [*laughter*].

I think my mom didn't finish 11th-grade year. She got her GED. My aunt did up to 10th grade. She went back to community college and got an associate's in accounting. My Aunt Sammy, I don't even think she made it to high school, and my uncle, he just went straight to the Army. He didn't 'cause especially the men had a hard time growing up, so college wasn't really a thing for them. My uncle, he finished high school. My uncle went to the Army. My mom just got her GED and went to be a corrections officer, and my aunt, even though she dropped out in 10th grade, she actually got back on her feet and she actually made something, she did something with her life.

Right now my aunt's actually unemployed. She's been unemployed for about two years since I was 17, and so about two years. Right now she does taxes and all. She's real good at accounting and health services, but right now she's going through her crazy state of mind. She's just home watching the kids. She has two twins—two babies.

K–12 Educational Experiences

Elementary school was Torres Elementary School. That was in Baltimore City, and I stayed there till the beginning of my fourth-grade year. That's public. Then I went to Hetzel Elementary/Middle School. That's also in Baltimore City. That's from fourth grade to sixth grade. My mom passed away in sixth grade, so seventh grade I moved to Mt. Claryville Academy in Baltimore County, and that's where I went to middle school. It was actually a really good middle school in Baltimore County, but it was also public. It was a magnet.[9]

My elementary school was all Black school 'cause I lived in the city, and my middle school—it was kinda both actually 'cause I lived in the Black part of Baltimore City, but it was also still a White neighborhood as well, so it was both Black and White. My middle school had a lot more diversity, 'cause it was a magnet school and I lived in Baltimore County. That's where everybody comes together. At my high school, I had never seen some of them people in my life. I'm serious. It's Polish, Russian people, Chinese students, African—like from everywhere. We had an ESOL program, so they let children from different countries come in. They were actually a lotta fun 'cause you learn new things.

Me and my sister, we was in the same classes every year until our fourth grade year, and she stole a wallet from the teacher. Nobody understood that, and then after that we been actually separated from schools ever since, and in fifth grade we were separated completely. She went to Gwendolyn Elementary/Middle School after stealing the wallet.

My third grade teacher was Mr. Gripple. He was my favorite teacher. He was my brother's fifth grade teacher. Then he got to the third grade and had me and my sister, so me and my sister used to make him mad *every* day. He'd be hitting the wall. He used to bang the wall when the class got upset, and I remember one day my mom came up there for parent-teacher conference and she went out on the date. It was like a friend date. They hung out and everything. To this day, he's my godfather.

Now he's my godfather. From third grade to now he's still in my life even when my mom passed away. He's actually been there more since she passed away. He comes to all my basketball games, my track meets. He came to all my cross country meets and everything, and I know right now he moved to Chicago and he writes me and my sister letters all the time and he's coming back down here this weekend to see my brother. So he's No. 1.

My second favorite teacher is Mrs. Corning. I remember seventh grade, we didn't get along. She was one of the worst substitute science teachers. She took her job a little too seriously man, you're substitute teacher! But, anyway, in ninth grade I walked into class and I was like, "Oh my God, I got this teacher again." She actually remember who I was. When she said my name, she said, "Tierra, you're in my class?" I said, "Yes." She said, "Oh, this is gonna be a fun year, evil thing," and yet she always made sure I had everything right. She knew about my mom and everything, so she always made sure I had everything so I didn't mess my grades up. People would say that you're not supposed to have a friendship with teachers, but I considered her more than a friend 'cause she'd tell me anything. I could tell her everything. I never hold anything back from her.

She always made sure I didn't do nothing bad in class and anytime I did, all my teachers would go back to her, and sometimes I'd walk down the hallway. She'd be like, "Tierra." I'd be like, "Oh, man, somebody told her," and she always on point with me. She knew me like the back of her hand, especially when I was with the guy I'm with now, Kamal, we used to argue all the time. She still was like, "Ya'll need to stop arguing." I don't know. To this day, she still talks to me. She's one of my favorites too. She only gave me a B [*laughter*]. I didn't understand it, but like I say, she's my teacher first and she gave me the grade I deserved, not the one I want.

Ms. Berkley was my least favorite teacher. Me and my man, the guy I'm with now, we've been together for five years since freshman year in high school. She always liked his older brother Irving. She always liked both of them 'cause Irving was a basketball star. He was a football star, and senior year he became a track star. So I had her from AP Statistics my senior year, and even in years before when I talked to her, she'd say hi and bye, but then in AP Statistics, she really just didn't like me. I felt I'd get a little up 'cause I'm

Kamal's girlfriend and I'm with the family. She didn't like me. She actually gave me an F my first semester when I did all my work. Then she gave me a D, and she just didn't like me. Every time I asked something she would say, "No." She said, "I'll give it back to you," and she'd forget, and she just didn't pay me any mind. She was really rude. Yeah, I didn't like her.

If I had to rank my high school experience between 1 and 10, I'd give it an 8. I take two points off 'cause some of the teachers, but I actually learned a lot, especially in high school. I met a lot of new friends. The school was nasty, but that's another thing. The whole environment of the school was actually a safe environment. We had cops so you know nothing really bad would happen. It was just, everything about the school, you had to love it.

Carver University

Carver, at least I would consider it, is a good track school. My college prep teacher in high school, she told me she went here, and I was like, "Really?" and I came on a college tour and I actually liked the campus, even though it was kind of out in the bushes, but I liked it. I wanted to come here as I came to see it and I met the coach, and I was like, "Man, I just really wanna come here."

My family really didn't have any say in it. They didn't really encourage me to come to Carver. They were just saying, "Just make sure you go to college," because our generation of my family were the first ones to ever go to college. My aunt's son was the first ever in our family to ever attend college, so us going to college it's like, "Do this for your mother. Do this for the family." We are the first generation, so we had to, so that was just about it. My aunt just encouraged me to go, not my choice.

I looked at another Historically Black College down South, and that's it. I wasn't really trying to go down south. I was into looking at HBCUs, 'cause I might get a minority scholarship, but I just think Black people should stick together [*laughter*]. I was gonna transfer to my sister's university because the coach was actually gonna give me a full ride to go. She was gonna give me a full scholarship. Right now I'm paying Carver in loans since I live in Maryland. They don't have me on grants, so that's the only reason why I was gonna go down there, and they actually have a special education program.

My grade point average right now is a 2.1. That's because I failed Mrs. S's class.[10] I did good in my other classes. It was just that one 'cause I only took 14 credits. I couldn't drop another class,[11] and with that F it just really messed up my GPA. I got one A, B, and C in the other classes and that—the F. This semester was pretty good, I guess 'cause last semester I wasn't playing around but I didn't take it as serious as I was supposed to. This semester I go to class, practice, and back to my room or go to the library, now that my computer is broke, I go to my room to try to do my work. Because since I've been eligible[12] and I can run track, I wanna actually have my name out there instead of being unattached.

Teaching Career

I actually wanted to go into law and then when I got to high school my whole views kinda changed. I was actually talking with my godfather, and he's like, "Political science is a good major, but what are you gonna fall back on out of political science?" So it makes you think, kinda. By tenth grade, I actually wanted to do special education as my major and political science as my minor, and my godfather's like—he said, "Political science is a good major, but that's not something to fall back on," so I'm just gonna stick with education and early childhood, just to try to stay in education. I didn't wanna be a secondary education history major because it's kinda boring. I like history and stuff, but after awhile it's like, "Okay. Well, time to change the subject. Get on to World War II."

I wanted to do special ed.[13] 'cause just the children I guess. I know with me personally, I had a cousin with special needs. My sister was always scared of him, but for some reason I always had a really special bond with him, and then one day—I was helping him make cereal and everything and he was like, "I love you." And that was the end of it like, "Wow. He said that to me."

When I was in 10th grade, 'cause I was always around them 'cause my school was a school for special education. They had their own floor and I always seen them in the hallway. I always talked with 'em. Then in high school I was a student leader over in the gym and I was helping out the special ed. children, and they really loved me. I never looked at them different. They were just like me. They just had a different special need than I did. I remember when it was time for me to leave 'cause I was a senior, I came back. They called for me like, "I missed you. Where'd you go?" I'm like, "I had to go," and then one girl gave me a high five. She's like, "We really missed you." It was like—I don't know. It was just something about the kids. I wanted to spend more time with them.

My aunt actually thought being a teacher was pretty good. The only thing she said was bad was, "You won't make a lotta money." A lotta people are scared of students with special needs. My aunt said personally she would never do it, and she said, "That's something that a lotta people. You got courage. A lotta people don't have that to be around children like that." My aunt actually thinks a teacher is there for a reason. They have a purpose of being a teacher. A student gets a certain teacher for a reason.

So then I had a next-door neighbor who was actually my sister's teacher. She's in special education. She was kind and everything. She said, "You can go to California. They have jobs." She was just telling me everything. She said, "If you ever need help, come to her," and my family thought it was actually a pretty good idea for me to do that.

I don't really think anything bad about teaching. I know teachers deal with what they think is bad potentially. We might not like it, but they are only doing what is gonna benefit us. I think the responsibilities of a teacher is to try to make sure students pass even though they may not want to, but make sure that you help them out by passing, and I think the environment of the classroom. Make sure it's also a good place to learn. If it was a boring classroom with nothing on the walls, nobody would be encouraged to actually do anything, and just the personality of the teachers.

I think the rewards of teaching is friendship. I personally agree, I think every teacher should get along with every student in the classroom, so if teachers do what they're supposed to do, at the end of the day then the students are gonna love 'em and they're gonna learn and have friendships with them. Some of the frustrations is all the work. Some teachers just go a little crazy on the work. I just think so. I think to grade the work. Teachers give a substantial amount of work to students and then some teachers never have time to grade 'cause they think more work is gonna benefit the child, but you're putting too much pressure on yourself. You gotta think both ways instead of just one way.

I know I'll be happy all the time as a teacher. I know I will never, ever be a mean teacher. I guess I would go around teaching anywhere. It doesn't matter where. Any grade I'm in I would like to teach. I wanna teach young students because the older classes—they really don't respect teachers, and if you can get 'em—you teach 'em young and teach 'em how to respect teachers, then they'll learn how to respect teachers when they get older. My ideal grade would be second grade, or maybe kindergarten 'cause they're so cute.

A typical day of teaching would be, we'd come in and have the pledge of allegiance. Then I would find out in the beginning of the year how their summer was going—on Monday, how was their weekend. Ask personal questions and not too deep 'cause they're young. Then probably do some work. In between, you might have a break time. They read a book or eat a snack or something, and then maybe color, and I'm gonna give them work, but in between you don't have them in their work all the time. Give 'em a break because it'd gotta be.

It may be hard my first year 'cause it's always rough the first year 'cause you just don't know. Student teaching will help you but when you're out there on your own it's a different story, so it might be rough my first year. It might take me a year or two to actually get down the kinks of it. Then I wanna get my master's in special education. I'm trying to go all the way with this.

After five years, I think I'll have teaching down. I won't be a master at it, but I'll have it. I'll know what to expect from a child afterwards. Twenty years from now? I don't know, to tell you the truth. I may go into administration after a couple years when I get tired, but I wanna be in education for a while. Maybe after 20 years, I'd go into administration because the more knowledge you obtain, the better you'll be coming into administration and stuff.

If I had to summarize teaching in one phrase, it would be "great." Every teacher is leading other people, basically.

Basic Skills Certification Exam

I don't see the point of the basic skills exams 'cause you have to take an exam. I don't understand why we're taking SATs all over again. That's my whole thing. We took 'em and now we have to take a test to become a teacher if we already have our degree. If we have a degree it's not gonna matter. The second teaching certification exam, that one's actually understandable. I think it's understandable. That's not bad. The first one is pointless.

I actually think my preparation for the basic skills exam is pretty good, especially the workshop and the books they gave us, 'cause it help—actually helps us think about what's gonna be on the test and go back to your other books and read and actually try to study, so the workshop has been good. Me and two other people from the track team actually study together. We have the track meet that day of the basic skills test and we're just gonna go—we actually study together to actually get the stuff down.

****

Tierra graduated from Carver University three years later, but not as an education major. Due to the basic skills and her GPA, she ended up switching majors to Human Services/Sociology. I ran into Tierra the year after her graduation, as she was at Carver supporting her friends' graduation that year. Tierra told me she went into a graduate program to work on her Masters in Social Work. Her goal is to be in Counseling Education working with children.

Tanya

"Yo! This new freshman Tanya is so official!" exclaimed my colleague and friend, Dr. Phillipe, one day in my office. He continued, "She just passed the basic skills exam her first semester. That's what's up!"

"For real! That's awesome!"

"To top it off, she also looks like your baby sister," joked Dr. Phillipe. The following semester, a beautiful woman walked into my Educational Psychology class. She was one of a few of our Secondary Education, Mathematics majors in the department and the university's star softball pitcher. Her curly hair, fair skin, and athletic build resembled mine in many ways, and I immediately knew this was Tanya. She, too, has a similar accent like mine as she came from a suburban neighborhood outside of Cleveland.

Home

I've lived in Cleveland my whole life. My parents both lived here. My mom actually grew up around the corner, and my dad grew up down the street. My grandparents still live in their same houses. So everybody's still there, except for maybe a few of my older cousins that moved to DC.

Well this year was my parents' 26th anniversary, so I guess they were married young. They were 25. My mom's turning 50 this year so they were 25 when they got married; 25, 29. They were high school sweethearts. It was weird. I think my dad had already graduated from high school; maybe a year. My mom and her best friend were walking to summer school, and my dad was like trying to pick her up. Like, "Oh, you're really cute." So they were dating ever since then. It really is cute. It's hilarious [laughter].

I think he waited for her for college or he was there maybe a year before her. I don't know the particulars about college, but I know they met in high school. My mom was a senior, and they went to college together.

Then my dad, Ivan, he went to Titan University also with my mom. He graduated from Smith High School, and he graduated from Titan University. I don't know what his major was, but he owned his own business and now he's working with construction, like commercial. He stopped his business in building homes because how things [the economy] going down. He was a contractor. So he really wasn't doing too well so he's just working with commercial work. He's working on the airport; they're renovating it. So his company's working on that so he's the project manager of everything they're pretty much doing.

My mom is Lola. She went to Titan, and she actually went to the high school I graduated from and then she went to Titan for, I think it was a year. Then went to Washington and got her something with CPA, certified public accountant. She's the chief financial secretary at a university; she works under the chair for campus services. So she deals with the police. He's the vice president. He works with all the police, the food; all that kind of stuff he does. She does reports to him and then to the CFO. She works under both of them. She works with them.

Then she's the head of two committees, which I don't know what they are, but she's always complaining about the minutes. So I know that much. Everybody asks what she does. I really couldn't tell you.

I was born in '90 and my mom was born in '59. So my mom was in her 30s when she had me. Then my brother, Ivan Jr., is 23. He just turned 23. He goes to the Art Institute. That's where he's graduating at the end of March. I think he's doing graphic design. My brother and I are the only two.

K–12 Educational Experiences

I went to public school. I went to Johnson for kindergarten. I went to Fairfield, which is in my town, and I went to Langley High School. Our school's really small. We have a really small community and mostly like 90% of it is Jewish. I lived in a Jewish community so I had a lot of synagogues around, temples, all that. So it's mostly Jewish. In elementary school, like kindergarten through, I really couldn't tell you up to when, I was one of maybe three African Americans in my whole grade at least.

Then finally people started coming because the housing went down. There's a lot more rentals and stuff like that. Like an apartment. There's a mall right by the city, so there's a lot of apartments around the mall that African Americans moved into. But for a while we were mostly just four or five, six African Americans.

I graduated high school with 160–170 people. Still quite a few Jewish, obviously. They just weren't gonna move out. Then we had graduated with maybe 15 other African Americans, a few Asians, a few Indians. Their parents are from India and then maybe a few people from Russia, but very few, like two, but most of it was Jewish. I don't think it really mattered being one of the only minorities because that's what I'd grown up with. It's like I flowed right in. I just adapted to the situation, I wasn't gonna act up, like my parents told me, "Don't ever act up no matter what," so I wasn't gonna do that. I just pretty much would slide in. I made friends with everybody in all of my three schools.

My best friend, she lives directly across the street. I went through kindergarten with her. She's the only one I can remember that I actually went to kindergarten with. So actually my two best friends that I went all the way through school with, but all the Jewish kids, I always went to school with them, but people I actually hung with outside of school there was only two of us that I can remember all through K–12.

After pre-K and kindergarten, then we had Johnson Elementary, which was first through third. Then Fairfield was fourth, fifth, and sixth. Then middle school was seven, eight. High school was ninth, 10, 11, 12. Eventually they changed it. Sixth, seven, eight for middle school. Ninth through 12th. But they just changed it after I graduated. I really couldn't tell you why they chose to do that because our middle school's not big. Like only having 150 students in each grade. We didn't have a big middle school so they're really not like all the middle school teachers. Even the students feel it's too crowded. They might change it back.

In elementary, it was a lot of teachers teaching you and you have projects about it. I remember we had a research paper in the fourth grade. We had a research paper and so you had to present it to the class, so it was a lot like they tried to throw those on every year.

Then fifth grade we had more group projects because we watched *Roots*. That was awkward, but we watched *Roots* and we had a big group project with that. Well, in that grade there was two of us, African Americans, in my actual class. So, there was this—I don't know. When we saw the people getting whipped and then saying the N word, all the kids were shocked to hear it, but I knew it was coming. So it was just an awkward situation because as soon as they would say the word it felt like all eyes would be on us and we were girls.

So we'd always just sit in the back and everybody'd just turn around as soon as they said it or something. But our teacher was African American so that helped because he helped us through it and said, "If you guys ever need to leave the room, don't worry," kind of thing.

Then every year after that we kept working on projects. Now when we got to seventh grade we had a really big Holocaust project because we went to the Holocaust Museum so we just had to prepare for that.

Then high school everybody's teaching was different. My English was a lot of group projects all through high school, and we did some credit seminars pretty much what we were doing. Then with my social studies, it was more like research based. You had to find what was the history of this country and stuff like that. So it really just depended on the teacher, but it was a lot of research, group projects and lectures because Wednesdays and Thursdays we'd have block scheduling so every class was an hour and a half. On those days, we'd have longer lectures, and we'd take a lot of notes.

We had block scheduling in high school 'cause they wanted us to get used to it, which I agree. It really helped me because now I can actually sit through an hour and 20 minute class and keep focused because before I don't think I'd be able to. High school, it was so hard for me, but now that I had to go through three years, I'm like whatever. It's another day I gotta go through. And in our high school—no, in all our schools we have a big deaf community because they bused into our schools and learning disabled, like physically handicapped, mentally handicapped, everything. We have programs for both of those. The sign language interpreters would come if the students came to class. If they were in my class they'd be there, but I honestly didn't have a lot of classes with them. I didn't have any classes with physically handicapped and mentally handicapped. They had their own classes. They weren't really integrated into ours. The deaf students were, though. A lot of them have hearing aids. They're not totally deaf so they can hear and they don't really need an interpreter. I think I only had maybe one class with an interpreter in it in my whole high school career.

Elementary through fifth grade, I was just an average student. I cared what grades I got, but I never really took the time to really care. Seems like we had gifted programs all through school. Like GT, gifted and talented. So a lot of people were in that, but I never really cared to be in that. I was fine with my gifted and regular classes.

Then in middle school it got worse. I really didn't care, and I was doing bad. I never had to go to summer school or anything, but I wasn't putting in effort. I was getting Cs and if I just passed the class, it's okay. Then freshman year hit me and I was like, "Oh, I actually gotta work." I did really bad freshman year English. I got a D in it, but, I don't really like English. So, I did really struggle with English so I did really bad and that's what hurt my GPA all-in-all because senior year came and I was like, "Oh wow, I really can do this." I tried hard. I got all As and Bs in all my classes. So I was like, "Why didn't I do this before." So finally it kicked in.

Once I started applying for school like junior year. I really need to do good in school to go somewhere and not just be stuck. So I finally got it together. Now I go back to my high school and talk to the younger kids because they don't really understand what they have to do to get into college. It's a newfound freedom for them. They're just like, "Oh well, I'll just do what I did in middle school." That's what I did and, mm, no. So I try to go back to tell them "You really do need to focus. Your freshman year is the most important." Honestly, I feel it's the most important year of high school because if you don't do good, it's so hard to bring your GPA up. You could just be out of luck for the rest of your career, pretty much.

My American Sign Language teacher was really influential. This was 10th and 11th. She just helped me through. If I needed something, she was there. All through high school, one of my social studies, Mr. Dooley, he was just really laid back, if you need anything. I could always talk to him about everything. He was really big on the achievement gap in Detroit and all through Ohio, or Cleveland actually. So he was really big on African Americans, like, "If you need anything, you could come to me." I email Mr. Dooley, my social studies 'cause he always is wondering how I'm doing and stuff. I actually keep in touch with my principal and vice principal because they were younger. So they always were wondering how I was doing.

Then my only African American teacher in fifth grade, Mr. Barnes. There was only two permanent African American teachers. Not saying music isn't a teacher, but then there was a music teacher that was African American. Then we had an Asian art teacher and that was it. We had helpers, like aides for special students, but that was three people.

Outside of school, I was vice president of Jack & Jill.[14] You can be born into Jack & Jill. First grade maybe was when I started. I wasn't really active then. My mom was just like, "Whatever. You do what you have to do." But then high school came, and for my brother, my mom was the senior advisor for high school. So once he got out she was like, "Okay, you can go to everything now." So I had to go to everything. I didn't mind. I liked it. I liked certain people, but there was only a few of them I actually talked to.

My mom knew a lot of the people that were in Jack & Jill before her. She had good friends that were in it before her. So that's who got her in it, but when she was younger she used to say she used to go to Jack & Jill parties and stuff. I think that's really what it was. That's why she wanted us in it.

I've been playing softball all my life, but serious playing probably seventh grade is when I learned how to play seriously, so I started pretty much seventh, eighth grade. I wasn't always a pitcher. I played other positions, but I never was really good at them I guess 'cause I never really wanted to put the time in to actually learn how to play. I loved the game, but I never put my time in. So then my dad was the coach of the team called RBIs and they went to Florida one year to play in the World Series against teams from Puerto Rico and so I was like, "Oh, I wanna do this now." So that's when I started becoming more serious and actually wanting to do it.

My dad's very un-athletic. His brothers are athletic. Because I'm a daddy's girl, and I've always been. He coached my brother, but my brother wasn't athletic. So my dad was like, "Well, you're not athletic. We'll just let you do your art thing." Then he gravitated toward me and I was like "Okay." I was young. "I'll play; whatever." So I think that's why he actually started coaching.

Softball really took up my life, especially in high school. Sophomore to junior year, I played on a league three team and I played ball winter, summer and played summer in three teams. So I was really always running to softball. I played volleyball. I always went to basketball games, football games. I love sports.

All through middle school I played volleyball. I never really liked volleyball, but that's the thing because I learned that I did a lot better academically when I was active in sports and stayed in school longer because if I'd go home, I'd just sit there. I was a latchkey kid and so I'd just sit there and not do anything with my life. Once I realized I would play volleyball and it would help me get my work done or I wouldn't be able to play. During the winter when I wouldn't play basketball or do anything, that would be when my grades were not good. So my parents wanted me to stick with volleyball.

Carver University

It was a decision to go to Carver, but it's because of softball at the same time. A lot of the other schools I was applying to I wouldn't have been able to play softball, and without softball I don't really know what I would do. Then I just wouldn't be active in anything.

So coming to a school where I could play softball helped my decision. Then I liked the small classes and I love being close to DC, Baltimore, Philly. Not too far from New York. So all the places that I'd want to work in the future, I was close enough to get to them, and to be on the East Coast.

Carver was what I expected it to be. I knew I was getting into with a smaller school. I knew it'd be more cliquish like high school once again, but I was expecting it to be more. Coming from a suburb and having a predominantly White school, I was wanting to go to an African American school, but not wanting to go to a big one. So I thought there'd be more people like me, but getting to know it, there are people like me, but there's not a lot. There's a lot of people from the city that are coming here. So that was the only thing. I knew it, but I didn't know it was this extreme. Other than that, it's cool.

I knew it was gonna be a small campus. I knew it was gonna be small classes, which I love because that's really why I wanted to go to a small school because I always went to a small school. So if I went to a big school, I'd feel like I'd be lost within the first day and not be able to understand lectures and stuff. So that definitely was good when I saw small classes.

Then I would call the education department is like a family. So you get to meet everybody. You walk in the office and see everybody. You get to know everybody. So I like that. Everybody is so helpful. If you really need anything, anybody will be there to help you. So that's the other thing that I really like.

I don't really interact with people outside of class. I know a few of them from choir things, but actually outside, no. I think I keep to myself it's because it's a culture shock, first of all with coming from a predominantly White school and then coming to a school with a majority of African Americans. Then in high school, my whole high school year I was the person that was there the whole time so everybody knew me. Then when new people came in, they would try to get to know me. I would have to try to get to know them. It's not hard for me to interact, but it's like I gotta find my pathway into finding people.

Teaching Career

None of my teachers actually made me wanna be a teacher. It was actually my family because my aunt is a teacher in middle school. My other aunt is a reading specialist to all schools. Then my uncle is a high school teacher. So I always knew I wanted to be a teacher 'cause I want to help kids. So that was the only profession I actually thought I'd like, and I love it now.

In seventh grade, we had a day to shadow whatever kind of professional we thought we'd wanna do and see if you'd actually wanna do it—so I shadowed my aunt and my uncle. So that's pretty much when I knew, but I knew for sure, but I think I really knew my whole life because I always liked helping kids. I always tutored my little cousin. So I knew that I wanted to help children. I just didn't know in what way and what form yet. So finally when I went to see them working with the students, it helped me.

I chose math because math's the only subject I'm good in, but when I see teachers that don't love the subject they teach, I feel that they don't teach it to their fullest ability. So I knew that I wouldn't go to teach science or English 'cause I wouldn't be wholehearted in it. So math, I loved it. I was really good in it, and I don't think there was really any other option. It was either math or science and I stopped liking biology and stuff, so I was like, "Math, here we come."

I chose secondary because I worked in a camp and so I worked with younger kids. I never got to work with older kids, and I just saw it'd be easier for me to work with an older child. Then it's not that I'm impatient, but the stuff that you have to learn, the fundamentals in elementary that wasn't what I wanted to teach. I just had a concrete theory. Like this is the way you do it and there's variations of the way you do it, but there's a set reason and rhyme to why you have to do it this way. Like adding, I wouldn't know how to help a student learn how to add because if you don't know how to add then you don't know—you know what I'm saying? That whole thing is not secondary.

My mom was happy that I wanted to be a teacher. My friends thought I was crazy because you don't get paid a lot. I don't really care about that. Then my dad was like—'cause his good friend is the superintendent and a CEO. He was like, "Well, you know you're not gonna be able to just stop at being a teacher. You're gonna have to get all your degrees and work your way up." I was like, "Yeah, I wanna do that, but I still want to help high school students." I don't wanna just straight and get my doctorate because that's just not gonna do anything because I don't wanna be a college professor right off the bat. So yeah, I wanna get my doctorate, but it's not gonna be right off. So he was like, "You just gotta keep working. Don't lose sight of what your furthest goal is." So he's supportive still.

I really just want to positively influence a child's life. That's my goal as a teacher. It doesn't even have to be through math. If I could help somebody through a hard time or get a child focused, that's really what I want to do. Obviously, I want them to learn math, but I want them to get something out of school; something that I didn't get out of school.

I want to work in urban schools for a little bit, but then I also wanna go back to a suburban school where there aren't a lot of African American teachers so the students will be able to relate to at least someone and they have a role model. Like I can do this. I could come out of this, work with them and actually be a good teacher or good student. So I just wanna help influence their life in a positive way. I do wanna go back to the suburbs and help students in ways pretty much that I wasn't helped in. We didn't have any African American teachers in high school.

My future classroom, well, I want it to be really interactive because I know that's how I learn best and I think with math, you can't just sit there and lecture to them and tell them this is how it's gonna be. You have to do more interactive, give more real-life situations on how to perceive the problem and the solution. So it's gonna be a lot of interactive, ton of group work. It's kind of hard to do with math, group work and a lot of homework. Homework is the key in math.

I wanna be close to the students where they feel comfortable enough to come to me after school and get help, but I don't wanna be too close where they think they can joke around and I'm just another one of their friends. I wanna still be an authority figure, but I want them to know they can actually talk to me if they needed something serious.

Then with the other teachers, I want more of a collaborative team. Like all the maths are together, so it actually flows because in high school—they flowed, but they didn't at the same time. I want everything to flow where all the teachers, like you pick up exactly where from the last teacher left off or you do a little bit of review, then keep going because sometimes I felt like I missed some things in some classes and then the next year I was just like, "We learned that? Really?" but they never went over it. So I wanna do that.

Then with the parents I definitely want them to be more involved with their students and actually know what we're learning about. If they have questions about what we're learning about so they could help their students, it would work. So they wouldn't have to feel like they were stupid in a sense because they can't help their child. I want them to be able to help them, too.

Actually, when I get out of Carver I want to do Teach for America in some city; doesn't really matter. I would prefer to stay on the East Coast, but anywhere in Texas; that's fine. So I just wanna do Teach for America, get my master's and get teaching experience, while doing all of it. They'll help you pay for your master's and to get work experience in an urban environment.

I don't know what I want to get my master's in. I didn't really think of that. Not really sure. I wanted to do something along the lines of becoming administration, like become a principal or something. Yeah; something along those lines because I wanna be a teacher all my life, be able to teach every day, but I also want to do other things with my education.

Five years out from graduation, I wanna be in DC, Baltimore, teaching, have my master's, teaching and loving what I do. That's it. Teaching in the city still. Ten years out, I might have gravitated out toward the suburbs by now and I might have moved into the Carolinas, a little bit further down; warmer weather, but teaching more in the suburbs so that the students can get what I didn't get more of, like helping African Americans in a predominantly White school. Twenty years—I have no idea; I'll be 38. I guess, I'm still teaching. Probably by this time, I think I'm gonna be working on my doctorate and trying to either become a professor, maybe? Maybe become a professor, working more with administrative things. Could be a principal. Could be something working my way up to professor or superintendent. Not that I'd wanna be a superintendent, but a superintendent somewhere in there to help like all the schools; not just one area.

I want to have a set job before I get married—not get married, but have children at least because I want them to have a good household like I had, something that is a cohesive household. I just want structure all through their life. I don't want it to be me working all the time and not being able to be there for them. So I wanna be able to be more lenient and stuff like that with them.

****

Tanya continued to be one of the top students at Carver University, and she made a name for herself on campus as a great softball pitcher. Sadly, this all came to a halt the beginning of her junior year. She got into a car accident in October 2010. Tanya sustained major injuries, which permanently ended her softball career.

Without softball and the scholarship money, Tanya had to transfer to a university back in Ohio. She is currently majoring in Middle Childhood Education with a concentration in Mathematics and Science. Due to the accident and issues with the transfer of credits, Tanya's graduation was delayed twice. Currently, she plans to graduate in fall 2013.

Although freshman year was hard for Tanya to make friends at Carver, she did establish a core group of friends. She even drove in from Ohio to support and cheer on her friends' graduation at Carver.

· 4 ·

SOPHOMORE YEAR: ENTERING TEACHER EDUCATION

Dashawn

"Now Dr. Mawhinney…" This was often Dashawn's indicator that he was about to tell me a story, and it would often have me rolling with laughter at some point. Dashawn was a storyteller and a talker with a sense of humor, a combination that often made for great entertainment in any conversation with Dashawn. The story would then be delivered with his thick Baltimore accent and energetic personality. Thus, it is no surprise that Dashawn was the heart of Carver University. He was involved in many organizations on campus.

    I was fortunate enough to have Dashawn in three classes during his tenure at Carver University. He was a dual major in Secondary Education/Mathematics and Computer Science. Dashawn was one of the top students in the Education Department. Unlike other preservice teachers who continually struggled with the basic skills certification exam, Dashawn passed it on the first attempt. In the math portion of the exam, he got only one question wrong. With his passion for math, Dashawn would often tutor his peers for the math section of the basic skills certification exam. As a proud Baltimore County resident, Dashawn was already committed to urban education, as his story starts there.

Home

I have a mother and a father. We're always together, and I have an older sister. She's 24; and she just got married; and I have an adopted brother. He's my cousin, but his parents, unfortunately, passed away before he was legal. My mother was next of kin; so she adopted him; but he doesn't live with us. James lives with my grandparents. I'm 20. He's four months older than me. He goes to Carver as well, majoring in Mass Communication. He wants to be a sports reporter for ESPN. That's like his ultimate dream.

So James's mom was my mom's best friend, and then James' father is my mother's brother. We were all really, really close. His mother passed away before I was born. He was born in May. His mother passed away in August 'cause that was my mother's best friend. So that sent my mother into premature labor, so she had me in September when I was supposed to be born in October. And then his father passed away within the year, five days before Christmas. So we were always, always together; and my immediate family's really close. My mother's side, we're all really close. We have Sunday dinner and stuff like that.

My family lived in the city; but as soon as I was born, we moved to the county. So I've always lived in Baltimore County in the same house since I was three. I think they thought that it was better for us [in the County], to bring up kids in. When my parents met, they was in the same math class; and my father saw my mother; and she was sleeping in class. Here's how the story goes. She was sleeping in class, and my father teased her after class. You know, said something smart about her sleeping; and that's how they started talking; and ever since then, you know, they started going out.

Then they went to college together. They got a job because they got married, and then you know how it is when you get married. They got married, and then my mother got pregnant not too long after that. So they both got jobs. But that's pretty much how they met in high school. My mother wants to go to college, and I don't think my father has any aspirations of going back to college.

But my mother, her ultimate dream would be to be a music teacher for elementary school. Right now, she's a daycare worker. She works for the four- and five-year-olds. She works with a prekindergarten-type program. And my father, he used to work for a mailroom, and now he drives the disability buses that take people from their houses and stuff. He drives those in Maryland, so he works for the government.

And my sister, she graduated with a bachelor's in psychology, and now she goes to [an HBCU] grad school right now to get a master's in psychology. And she works right now for Social Security. I don't know exactly what she does, but I know she gets paid really well 'cause she works for the government. I know she's not doing what she wants to do; but she said as soon as she gets her master's. She just got married, and she's pregnant. You know, so she's about five weeks pregnant now. So I think she's gonna stay until the baby comes, and then, you know, switch 'cause she gets paid really well, and my brother-in-law, he works. He's a mechanic, and he just graduated from school.

K–12 Educational Experiences

I went to pre-K, and I actually started school early. My mother got me in that way because my birthday's in September. So, technically, I didn't reach the age deadline. I was turning four that month, so she got the school system to let me come in.

So I went to pre-K and I absolutely adored my pre-K teacher. But I remember that it was one pre-K teacher that was so mean and you could hear her yelling at her kids from inside our classroom. And I was kinda like, "Oh," you know what I mean? Like I was kinda scared of her. Everybody was scared of her. Even up till fifth grade, I was a little terrified of her, and then I went to kindergarten.

I went to Whitefield Elementary School. You can walk there and get there in about two minutes from my house. So I live right there, and the school's right there. It's a public school. And then the pre-K program was set up where you would enter the school for half a day. Then they had two separate pre-Ks. They had morning pre-K and afternoon pre-K. I went to morning pre-K because my mother worked night shift at that time.

And then I went to kindergarten when I was four, about to turn five. I always turned after I was already in that grade. Kindergarten, I don't really remember much about kindergarten, except for we got naps and stuff like that. I learned my name in kindergarten and all that stuff. In kindergarten, I remember that every day you came in, you had to find your name out of this bin; but it looked like a bookshelf. You had to find your name and you had to find today's date, and it was something else you had to find. You had to pull 'em out and put 'em in your own specific slot each day you came in so it teaches your name and all the different stuff. That's all I remember [*laughter*].

First grade, I loved my first-grade teacher. Her name was Ms. Collard and she was a really nice older White lady, the typical White lady—she was just like a librarian. And one of the things I remember about first grade that's still in my head till this day. Because we was learning about animals, and one of the activities we got to make an aquarium. We made it outta bread, and we used blue cream cheese as the water and we had the little goldfish and we had something on—it was something green, like supposed to be the seaweed. I forget what was the green element. And then we got to eat it afterwards. It was really nasty, but it was really fun to make 'cause goldfish and cream cheese and bread sticks never go together. It was a great activity. It was fun to make, and I still remember that to this day. I remember it like I did it yesterday.

Well, I didn't really enjoy my English teacher for fourth grade because his expectations seemed like a lot for us. So fourth grade, I felt myself trailing off a little bit because of all the work he gave. It was just a lot to put on a fourth grader. But other than that, I absolutely adored my elementary school. It was a great school. Everybody got along. All the teachers were really nice, for the most part, except for that one lady. The kindergarten teacher that everybody was scared of. Everybody else, all the other teachers were pretty good.

The school was about 95% African American. Of course, the neighborhood I grew up in about is 95% African American. But all of our teachers, as far as teachers go, we had about 70% Caucasian people and about 30% African American. I only had two male teachers outta all the years I went there. It was about maybe 500, 600 students. Each class was about 25–30-ish. That was about the average class size.

I then went to a magnet middle school, which is a public school, technically, but you have to apply to get in. It's a public school, meaning if it's your zone school, you could go to it. But if you're outside of the zone, you had to apply. And everybody had to apply for a magnet, inside the place. The magnets were performing arts, visual art, math and science, and foreign language. So those were the four magnets, and performing arts was the only magnet where you had three concentration areas. Everybody else, they had their own—like math and science, you have the math and science was your magnet. Meaning you had a lot to do with your magnet, which could be anything from drama to Spanish. But in performing arts, you had a magnet, a minor, and elective.

So my magnet was orchestra. My magnet was a performance arts magnet, but my specific magnet was orchestra because I played the violin. I learned the violin in elementary school. So I went there for orchestra. I really wanted to be drama. My minor was drama, and my elective was Spanish. And that school was a pre–high school, which means like a lot of our eighth-grade work was the work at the high school level. For example, my Spanish class, I took Spanish I and II in high school. I got credit for it, but I didn't know I got credit for it. That's a different school, but I didn't know I got credit for it in high school. So I took Spanish I and II again; but when I got a better counselor, I was informed that I already took it in middle school and got the credit for it. So I didn't have to take it again.

For my magnet, you had to audition. So I had to play a song. I had to play a song, and then I had to sight read, and then I had to play my scales all the way up and down, but my magnet was really easy to get into. So almost anybody that applied for orchestra got in because there's not that many people interested in string instruments. You see what I'm saying? So most of us got in. But like drama, you had to act out a scene. We had to do a little bit of improv, and that magnet, specifically, was more cutthroat. We had a dance magnet, too. Stuff that was more cutthroat. My sister and my brother all went to this middle school. So my sister went there first. My sister was dance, band, and her elective was, I think, foreign language, as well. My brother went for visual arts and his elective was Japanese.

And then that school was really well, and it was very diverse. It was about 65% Caucasian; I would say 15% Asian, and then maybe the rest of it African American. So the African American group population was small, fairly small in the school, but it was good because I went to a mostly Black elementary school. So it was good to, you know, experience different cultures and different backgrounds. You know how some schools, it's very cliquish because there's such a small percent of African American students. They would all clique together, but everybody kinda got along with everybody. Everybody hung out with everybody.

I really enjoyed that school, and I learned so much. I learned a whole bunch in that school. One of my favorite things is eighth grade; and every eighth grade, no matter what your magnet was, we did, for three weeks, we read *The Giver*. That's one of my favorite books now. Me and my mother read that book together when I was in eighth grade, 'cause my parents always helped us with our homework. So when we had reading and stuff, they would read the books with us, make sure we understood it, probably up until high school. So my mother read the book with me, and we absolutely adored the book.

The only thing that I didn't like about that school is, it was challenging; and so you really had to stay on top of it. Sometimes we got a little discouraged because we weren't aware that we were doing high school work. So we would get a little discouraged 'cause we didn't understand it or didn't grasp the concepts; but what we didn't know until after we graduated is that the teachers couldn't fail you out of a subject. There was no way you could get a F in any course, you always get a passing grade, C or above. And the teachers knew. They knew that you was doing high school work, so they were a little bit more lenient with you, so you could grasp the concept.

When I went to high school, I went to Baltimore Academy, which is just a regular public school. I felt like I was in middle school all over again. I was ahead of everybody else. When I was in Algebra I, I did that in seventh grade. And I was like, "Oh, this is easy." So I was always on the honor roll. Because of middle school, I got into honors trigonometry, a whole bunch of different honors courses at my high school because we already learned the basics. So when I got to high school, it was kinda like, "Well."

The bad thing about that is my high school was kinda bad. You know what I mean? Like it was kinda a rough school, if you will. Right now, they have metal detectors; and they have a system where you swipe in to go to class. So if you skip and you swipe in the next day, a big alarm sounds, at their station, and you have to go to the office. So it was kinda bad, a bad school; but I really didn't learn anything there 'cause I learned it all in middle school. And the only reason I went there 'cause it's my zone school. At that time, I didn't feel confident enough to apply to the school I wanted to go to, which was the big sister school to my middle school. It's called County. And that's a performing arts school, as well. I was scared to apply to County because, I guess, I was just doubting myself, and I guess I was more afraid of the rejection letter. You know what I mean? And then I never really expressed it to my parents that they were able to push me to do it. So I just like let it go by the wayside and went to my local high school. Plus, my brother was going to County, as well, so I was like, "Well, I'll just, you know, go to the school." And my sister went to the same school as well. She was alumni.

At County, I coulda continued doing orchestra and stuff like that. I wanted to go to Western 'cause I knew my high school didn't have an orchestra, and I wanted to continue my violin aspirations. Going to my middle school, we really developed your skills in violin playing and now it's like I don't even play my violin anymore. It just sits in my room in the little corner. Just few years ago, I was volunteering at an elementary school. I just donated it. They had a string program there. I used to tutor there, and I was like, "Here, just take my violin 'cause it's just collecting dust." My high school was predominantly

Black, and they didn't have orchestra at all. So I was forced to learn another instrument because I wanted to keep up musically. Which was a good thing, 'cause I got into the marching band and I started my love for marching bands and stuff like that. I play the trumpet now.

My high school graduating class was 300, and I think we started with maybe 350, 400. So it was pretty big. You know, 300 each class. School's at 1,200 students. It's a nice two-story building. We had a football field, three baseball fields, so we're kinda big. In Baltimore, you have people who are using family members' addresses to get into county schools. Sometimes you get the people who, for whatever reason, in the city, you have to act, you know, a little bit tougher coming to county schools and having that same mentality. So it's turning the county schools bad, as well.

But I remember one teacher, it was math, and it was high school. His name was Mr. Lee and this is why I despise geometry to this day because he taught teacher-centered, which he just taught straight out of the textbook. If you go ask him a question, he will ask you, "Did you read the textbook?" And if you said, "Yeah," then he was like, "Well, really, 'cause you'll see on page so-and-so, the answer's right there." But he would never explain anything to you. It was just go to the textbook, read the textbook, go to the textbook.

But then I had some teachers who—like we had discussions. You know, they wanted our input. I'm that type of learner, though, I'm a very visual learner. And I have a semi-photographic memory. So a lotta times, especially in high school and even sometimes in Carver, I don't have to study for things. Like I see it and see how the teacher did it, I can reproduce what they did. So even the one with the textbook, his class was hard because he didn't show me how to do it. I never saw him go through the steps, so I never grasped it. But a lot of my other classes, I got the concepts. I got great grades. Some of the classes, you get. So it's kinda hard to say which ones were teacher-centered, which ones student-centered, but I know the ones that were my favorite was student-centered.

For example, my history teacher, her name was Ms. Hardy—she was one of my mentors in high school. She's the one who kinda encouraged me to go to college—that I could do bigger and better things. In her class, she gave a lot of work, but we did a lot of group comments where we had to present. This was tenth grade. So she was really like the main teacher that got us to do presentations and present as a group. She would lead discussions. We did discussion about what we read. She let us be more independent. She didn't baby us. She didn't spoon-feed us the information. She let us go out and explore for ourselves. And then if we interpreted something wrong or they didn't get the right answer, then she would explain to us how you would go about getting that answer. I got to TA for her my senior year.

I became more and more bored in high school as the years went on. In Baltimore, you only have to take three maths, I think three sciences. You have to take four Englishes. So a lot of the course kinda sorta ends your junior year. And then your senior year is all electives. But one of my periods, I was TAing. So you really don't have to take that much your senior year. That adds to the boredom, and I took a whole bunch of classes senior year. I took a computer class where we just learned how to type in Microsoft Word. We got a typing class. I took a cooking class. I took dance. I TAed. I had an English, and the only other hard class I had was honors trigonometry, and that's because of my guidance counselor. She was new to the school, kinda sorta like persuaded me to take this 'cause she knew I wanted to be a math teacher in my senior year. She was like, "Well, it would look really good. You know, you're about to go to college. Why don't you take honors trig?" So I was like, "Okay." So honors trig, I really loved it. It was really fun, and I'm glad I took because I did get placed into pre-calc when I got here. But everything else, it was just a waste of time. I'm just taking it because I have to take something. I graduated 22nd in my class out of 300. I ended with a 3.4 GPA. The only reason why I was a 3.4 is 'cause of that geometry class in sophomore year. I got a C in that, so it kinda brought it down. I think I got a C in some other class—but it was really easy to get good grades in high school for the most part, especially 'cause I went to my middle school. And then a lotta places, if you didn't even try, you still would get a B by just showing up and sitting there. Middle school was more challenging. I managed to pull more Bs than As in middle school.

I did marching band in high school, and I've been in my drama ministry at my church. I've always been in drama ministry in there since I was in middle school. Other than that, I really don't have too many extracurricular—I hate playing sports. I spend most of my time on the computer, playing games, you know, doing stuff like that. Hanging out with my friends outside, but as far as extracurricular, just drama ministry and the marching band when I got to high school.

The main reason that I dreaded going to Carver and going to a college, too, because my parents pushed us to go. Go, go, go. But if we didn't go to college, they wouldn't be upset. It was one of those type of thing where it was ultimately up to us, but they pushed us in the right direction. Well, Mr. Garry, he was my teacher in high school. He started off as a substitute, and then the next year, he got a job as an English teacher 'cause I think he was going to school to get his degree at the time or something like that. So he's the one that paid for my application fee for Carver. I applied to Carver and four other HBCUs.

He invested in me 'cause he believed in me. I think all young men need a strong, another man to look up to 'cause we always have lots of women in our lives, thousands of women in our lives, but to have another young man that was kinda, sorta close to our age that we could look up to. We could go to him any time, and he would lend an ear, sit down and talk, even if he's rushing. He would have you walk with him and tell you what the problem is. So he's really the one that was really influential in my life.

Carver University

Well, James's father passed away five days before Christmas our senior year, he already didn't have his mother. His whole life that was his only parent. So I knew that I wanted to stay with James wherever he went for college. He wanted to go away to college, go out West. I didn't want us to go away. So for us to go away, especially with the loss, it would just be too much, I think, for both of us 'cause it was like me losing a father, too.

So we went to a college fair. That's the one good thing my high school provided was bus transportation to the college fair at Baltimore City Collegiate Center, and we went there, and we saw Carver. And the one thing that grabbed us is that they were starting a marching band. I don't want to brag, but our high school was the only Black band in Baltimore County that is very well established. And my bandleader went to another HBCU. He taught all those colleges, so he has connections everywhere. So he gets us good scholarship money to go to other schools. I was supposed to go there, but James wanted to go to Carver 'cause his father was an alumni here; and so I decided to come with him. Carver's kind of a legacy in my family; 'cause his father went there. My cousin our older cousin, she's like 60 now. She went to Carver. Another cousin that's like 54 now, she also attended Carver. So there's a little bit of legacy in my family to go to Carver.

So we decided to come to help start the band, and teaching is everywhere. My major's everywhere. So it wasn't a problem if I had to go to that school 'cause it just had my major. Now that I'm at Carver, I love it. I like certain departments more than others [*laughter*]. Like the Computer Science Department, I love. The Education Department, I love. The Math

Department, they have really smart people, and they help you out. So I think Math Department–wise, they can socialize people more, but I love the small school setting where you get to know everybody. We're all like a big family.

I'm doing college by myself. My parents can't afford to send three kids to college. So everything that I don't get in scholarship, I'm paying for myself alone. It's the same for James, out-of-pocket. Fortunately and unfortunately, he got a lotta money when his father passed away. So all the money from him being a benefactor is going to his college tuition, and he gets half off 'cause his father's alumni. And my sister, she pays for everything herself with student loans too. My parents, being a daycare worker and a bus driver, they don't really get that much money; and they do what they can. I have a job on campus, and I'm a student leader. We get paid for that. But I never get discouraged. I was raised in a strong faith household. I know the money will come from somewhere. I know there was always some way.

But, I'm the president of the marching band. I'm part of the Boys to Men mentoring. I'm the president of drama ministry on campus where I write the plays for the drama ministry and direct them and produce them, and they act it out. Unfortunately, for the last two years that I've been here, I have to act in the plays, as well 'cause we never have enough young men. But this year, we have enough people now. Boys coming in. I'm a tour guide in my free time, and I'm a tutor for the freshman cohort.

So I think the teacher program is really good; and I think that everybody in it pushes you into the class, pushes you take the basic skills exam, pushes you to take this class, pushes you there. And then when you do something well, it's always a lotta of pats on the back, which is good encouragement. In fact, when I passed the basic skills exam, I didn't know how all y'all found out about it—like that fast! So it's very encouraging. Everybody's very encouraging in the department. So I love the program.

I think of almost everybody in the program, we all talk outside of class. If we have something to do [class work] for one of y'all, we'll discuss, you know, like, right now, we're in Dr. Edgar's class; so we're like, "Did you finish your program?" You know what I mean? We'll help each other out.

So I'll sometimes go help out Virginia because she doesn't really grasp the educational technology concepts all the time. So I'll help her out. Like Tyrone will help me out with my English 'cause I have horrible grammatical errors all the time and mechanical errors. So Tyrone will proofread them for me, make sure everything's okay. So everybody in the Education Department are very helpful. They help each other, and we all, whether y'all know it or not, we all go out and recruit the freshman. See, if we even think we heard somebody maybe mention the education program, we're like, "Oh, you're about to be a education major? Come on." You know what I mean? Like we try to get more and more people to join the Education Department.

Teaching Career

I've always wanted to be a teacher since I was three. Well, you know how your parents asked you, "What do you wanna be when you grow up?" And most kids like cowboys and stuff like that. I've always wanted to be a teacher. I think it's just something I was born with, like I think I was destined to be a teacher. When I was in elementary school, my parents bought me one of them little teaching kits for kids, you know, with the little chalkboard, and I had a grading book inside of it and stickers and stuff. And my father and my grandfather and me used to play school. And my mother and my grandmother would be the principal and vice principal just in case I had to send 'em to the office [*laughing*]. But we always played school.

I just always wanted to teach somebody, help somebody else out. Even like when I'm out here in college now, I tutor on the side whenever I have a spare moment. I'll tutor people. I just like helping people out. I was a camp counselor over summer, and I loved that job. I taught 10th to 11th graders. But it was an educational camp, so I really got to teach. We had a theme for each week, and they had to do lessons. Just as long as I can remember, I was always going to be a teacher.

I wanted to be a math teacher since 11th grade. Before that, I wanted to be a English teacher. Before that, I wanted to be a elementary school teacher. I want to be a math teacher because, one, it's like a stereotype that African American males aren't good at math, and I don't believe that. I just believe sometimes you can be a self-fulfilling prophecy. You have self-fulfilling prophecy where you say, "Okay, everybody else is saying I can't do it. Then I can't do it." And then I've always done really well in math. Like I was in honors trigonometry, I got an A in that class. So I've always learned exceptionally well in math. It's never really come hard for me. So I thought that it would be good for young students to see an African American male who can teach them math. You know what I mean? So they can say, "Okay, well, I can do it. If he can do it, I know I can do it, too." Plus, English is boring. No offense.

My mother loves it that I want to be a teacher. It's like a thing in my family to teach. My grandmother went to college, an HBCU. She didn't finish, either. She's like 70-something now, and she didn't finish, but she was going for English education. That was her degree. Like I said, my mother wanted to teach. My sister has done daycare since she's been in college and high school. She's always worked in daycare. So it was like just the thing, you know what I mean? It's in our blood to teach. But my parents absolutely adore the idea of me teaching.

You know you always get the couple of family members like, "Well, why you wanna teach? Well, you could be a major like computer science." So they're like, "You could do something with computer science. Make a whole buncha money in it. You could do this and make a whole buncha money. Teachers don't get paid anything." That's what you always hear. You constantly hear it, even from my current teachers, "We don't get paid anything. Why do you wanna be a teacher?" But you have to love helping the students. You have to do it for the students instead of for the money. And I believe the money will come from somewhere. There'll be enough for me to pay my bills.

My goals as a teacher, I think, would depend on what specifically I'm teaching, but I definitely want my kids to feel comfortable in the classroom where they can participate. When I was growing up, there's certain classes that you wouldn't participate in 'cause you might get shot down or the teacher might skip over you all the time when you're trying to raise your hand. I definitely wanna make sure I incorporate everybody into my classroom. I definitely want them to grasp the concepts and not just move on 'cause sometimes we rush through something.

I definitely don't wanna be one of the teachers that teach for assessment. I've had classes where it'd be like, "Okay, we have to take this MSATs," or whatever the Maryland standardized tests are. And they'll teach just for that. 'Cause we'll do all the questions that will be on the test and you don't have to really learn anything. I don't wanna be that type of teacher. I wanna make sure I teach the curriculum, at least I'll cover everything. Like, let's say, you've never seen pi before, and then the teacher would just leave the kids alone. He'll encourage them to think about different ways of doing it, but they would never give them the answer for about 10 minutes. Then they'll have each of the students come up to the board and put their answers on the board. So you see the different ways everybody thought. And then, of course, one of the ones will be the correct way to do it or the more accurate way to get their answer. So I definitely like that. I was thinking about how I can incorporate that. Maybe I can do it as a drill. My drill could be the unknown problem, and then the last thing could be explaining that problem. Then it would be here is the problem for the drill, and "How would you do it now?" And see if they did it a different way than I did it.

And I'm a kid at heart, so I like playing with stuff. So I'm definitely gonna have blocks. If teaching geometry, I'm gonna definitely have blocks so they can see different shapes. If I'm having Algebra, maybe have money, different things 'cause I love visual stuff. And I love things because the kinesthetic learners can touch it. You can move it. I definitely wanna incorporate that type of stuff in there.

I need to have a little bit of noise in my classroom. Not unnecessary talking, but a teacher says something that's exciting or you got something finally, and he's up there like, "Yea!" That type of stuff is good. Or when a student doesn't understand, and the student next to 'em will help them out. Like the way I wanna set up my classroom, though, I'm the type of teacher that loves the rows. The two—the rows of two. Two, two, two, two, two, two, two, two, two. Have three rows of two. I think that's when I was in class at school, I think that was the best learning environment. 'Cause if you wanna do groups of four, the two in front of you would just turn around. Then you always have like a partner next to you where if you don't understand something, you can ask your partner. So I think that's a more effective way than maybe a big line and circle-type thing, I hate the desks that are facing each other. Like the four desks that are all facing in 'cause it seems like the students aren't paying attention. When you're facing in, you're more likely to talk to somebody. You're face-to-face instead of facing me.

I hope to be the mentor that some of these teachers were to me. That if somebody needs somebody to talk to 'cause you never know what's going on at home. So if somebody needs that extra person to talk to, they could always come to me. Just somebody to look up to. That they can always know you're there for them. Always come in smiling, energetic. Might irritate some. My energy could be a little bit much at times, but I just wanna have that maybe not like father/child type relationship, but definitely a older friend that they can talk to.

I wanna be the teacher that calls somebody's parents sporadically because they did something well or to call 'em if their child needs help to remind 'em of different events we're having. I'm definitely gonna stay in constant contact with all parents, and I think that's possible nowadays because everybody has cell phones. Everybody has Internet access. You could shoot an email. You could call. So it's better to keep in touch with your parents nowadays. It's easier. So I definitely would shoot 'em emails, maybe do summaries of what we did in class so they know. Or if a parent had a question about, "Okay, well, do you give homework on Fridays?" Whatever the question might be, they know they can always email me, call me, or things like that.

I wanna teach the middle school, which is about 20 minutes away from my parents' house. It was just built two years ago. It's a beautiful school, and I would love to teach there for about 10 years. I'm teaching there, I wanna go to graduate school to receive my master's in computer science and education. After I receive my master's, then I wanna come back to Carver and teach Computer Science at Carver while I'm getting my doctorate completed for education. I haven't really decided what specific part for education, but I definitely wanna get my doctorate in education.

Teaching Computer Science, and I would love to maybe go back to some type of administration-type thing and maybe be a principal or a president of a university or something high up. I won't see that until like 20 years from now, 20, 25 years from now. I definitely wanna teach first and get teaching. Get into the classroom and start teaching. If I don't get into that middle school, I would love to teach at my old middle magnet school or any other school in Baltimore County. I really don't wanna teach in Baltimore City. I am going to apply to be a principal of the school in the city, though. But, as of right now, I've got my heart set on Baltimore County.

I want to teach in the middle school because I really dislike little kids. I don't dislike them, but little kids can be annoying at times. And I don't have the patience for little kids, the, "I have to go to the bathroom" or "He hit me." That type of stuff 'cause I worked with little kids for a week at my summer camp, and it was fun. They're more energetic. They're more loving. They're more attaching. But middle and in high school, most of the time in high school, the students are already set in what they wanna be. So if they're the bad student who doesn't care about school, for the most part, they'll continue to be like that. I just love adolescents. Like the pre-teens, and that's the age where you need to be guided the most. You know, maybe 'cause you're going through puberty. You're trying to find yourself.

So if you have middle school teachers that are guiding you, then I believe that you'll be more successful 'cause middle school prepares you for high school. High school prepares you for college. Well, you need a strong foundation in middle school to help you go through high school, and high school so you can go to college, and they can succeed in college.

****

Dashawn ended up being a powerhouse at Carver. He became the face of Carver, as he held a prominent and coveted position on campus. Moreover, he also joined a fraternity in which he is still active today. Dashawn's path landed him in Philadelphia with his student teaching experience, and he also successfully passed the second part of the teacher certification exam for Middle School Math. But, all Dashawn's progress came to a screeching halt when at the 11th hour from graduation, Dashawn found out he was two courses short (Calculus 3 and Math Analysis) for his Math Education degree. This was apparently the university's oversight. Since those courses were not completed, Dashawn did not graduate with his Math Education degree, but he successfully completed his Computer Science degree.

After graduation, Dashawn decided to stay and plant roots within the Philadelphia area. Although not certified, Dashawn did land a job in education after college. Through an email, Dashawn explained:

> I was a Before and After school teacher for 1st–4th grade, but I recently left that because of my admin ... I put in my two weeks because I felt I wasn't being valued. I am now working in the marketing department of a storage company helping them with their online files.

But, Dashawn's journey and vision to be an educator is still holding strong. Dashawn explained what the current journey looks like:

> I was the Director of my summer camp this year and will be going back. All in all I'm doing ok and still trying to make it as an educator. Money is the main issue standing in my way of teaching right now. All of the programs like Teacher for America and Teaching Fellows say I have too much experience so I'm in a weird limbo land as far as teaching goes.

Jessica

"Well, you can tell it's winter, as I'm starting to get into my light bright phase," exclaimed Jessica as she looked down at her arms investigating the loss of her summer tan. A beautiful biracial woman (half African American, half Puerto Rican) from New Jersey, Jessica was queen of catch phrases like "light bright." This really shaped and molded her humor and interactions with others. She would sit quietly in class, often blending into the background, but when you get her one-on-one, Jessica is fun, caring, and has a great sense of humor.

Jessica was an Elementary Education major at Carver University. Most of Jessica's close friends were also from the Education Department. She definitely approached college focused more on the academics verses the sororities or other social groups. Her friends often referred to her as "Jersey," and Jessica talked about her life growing up there.

Home

I live with my mother and my father and my middle brother, and I have an older brother who lives not too far from me. He has a wife and two kids. All very close—always have family functions and stuff like that. Me and my middle brother are 1 1/2 years apart and me and my oldest brother are about 12 years apart. There's a big age gap, but we still get along very well.

I'm from New Jersey in a little small town in central Jersey by the shore and been there all my life in the same house. My dad is originally from North Carolina, and my mom's been born and raised in New Jersey as well. And my dad, I feel like he traveled from North Carolina up to Jersey and worked in a fish market.

And our town is just so small. My mom has a lot of brothers and sisters, so she was always going to the store to feed everyone. One night she ran into the fish market, and she met my dad and ever since it's been kind of chemistry. They've been married for 25 years or so.

My dad is a truck driver for a company and mom's a sales clerk at Marshall's. Neither of them went to college. But my brother, he went to community college for two years, and he was going to be a cop, but then had a change of heart. But he owns his own business now and he's doing very well with that. His business is with glass and mirrors, and he does like tabletops, shower doors, mirrors. He's had that for, I want to say, about six years give or take. My middle brother, he works as a waiter, and he works with my older brother if he needs the help. I'm the first in my family to go to [4-year] college.

K–12 Educational Experiences

I went to primary school from kindergarten to third grade. All my schools have kind of been very diverse because my town is very diverse. It's Caucasians, there are Hispanics, there's African Americans. We were a group of different people. It's a very small town so everyone knows everybody, and the school is very kind of small.

I went to public school. I was in one school from kindergarten to third. I remember projects and stuff in K–3. I remember a lot of projects like pilgrims. We made a Thanksgiving dinner in class. Like Flag Day, I just remember making flags and stuff. So I feel like it was a lot of hands-on activity, but I do remember watching. I feel it was more kinesthetic, hands-on work.

My middle school was from fourth to eighth and then high school from ninth to 12th. My middle school was kind of small. I remember three eighth-grade classes that had about maybe 20, or less than 20, kids in the class. It wasn't too bad. Sixty with the whole eighth grade altogether. I liked it a lot that the classes were small. I feel it's a better learning environment. Not so much individual attention, but it's better for effective teaching. The classroom tends to be quieter, and you can tell the teacher has more control over the class. And it's easier to answer questions and whatnot. So I like the small class environment.

I feel like in middle school, I took not a lot of notes, but I feel it was time to get to learning once I got to middle school. I was in the classroom, the teacher was teaching, working throughout the book, following through the book. It was a lot of reading though. I remember in history we had to read a lot. There were stories we had to read in English, a lot of essays I wrote. Essays, writing, working out of the book, some homework, class work.

I thought I have a connection with teachers. I don't mean it to be a teacher's pet, but I feel there is always some kind of bond, the teachers and I. My fifth-grade teacher, Ms. Wannamaker, she stands out so much to me. I feel she made me to be the person I am today. She always sees my struggles, but she never let them defeat me. She was always there to support me, stick it out, and we're the best of friends today. I call her my big sister, my mommom, my second mom. She's always there for me at the end of the day.

Ms. Wannamaker taught me in fifth grade, fresh out of college, and she's been teaching ever since. She just finished getting her master's degree in administration, so she's working toward becoming a principal. But she had a big influence on me. I don't want to say I'm a quitter, but I just get very frustrated easily. And she would just look at it and try to break it down. She called me up the other day to see how I was doing in math. And when I go home, if I go home for the weekend, I call her and see how she's doing. I stop by her house to see what's going on, just to catch up on some times. But it's always been a friendly level with Ms. Wannamaker and I. It was when I was a nerd, and she took me to church one day and I was praise dancing at church with her. So anything I needed, she was always there.

When I got to high school, it was a regional school. Through elementary and through middle school, I was always with the same students. When I got to high school, more people were added. So it was different towns within the area that went, and it was more Caucasians, but you could still see the mix of people within the crowd. But it was a visual and performing arts school. We had a visual and performing arts section, so there were dance majors there were piano majors, graphic art majors and stuff like that. It was all one school. It had just different classes. If you were a major for dance, you'd have two periods designated to dance for that class, but you'll still be in regular high school. It was all one high school.

And if you went to the main schools within the area, you could just apply and you could get in. In order to come to my high school, they had to apply to a major. Some people did graphic arts or photography. But it was a lot of different people outside the main three schools. If you were from outside the district, you'd have to apply, interview, and stuff like that. I know someone that actually paid to go to our school because of our visual and performing arts. I think she was a dance major because she knew like, "Oh, this could take me far," kind of thing.

I had applied for creative writing, but I feel like the lady I handed my papers to didn't give the papers in. So I never got an interview or anything. But it was no big deal. I took it as an elective, and I did fine in it, but it was just like—let me get in, get my core classes, and get out kind of thing. Our school was a mini Carver, about 1,200 or so, but I graduated with about 260.

I feel like high school was different in classes. I feel like math, they gave us blocks because blocks help you with geometry, put these shapes together. I remember one time in geometry class we had to make a golf course. It was mini golf, and we made our own shapes and stuff, had to put in what shape is this and kind of what's the angle. And English, I wrote my first research paper my junior year in high school. I stayed with the teachers often because I was just like, "How am I going about this?" They were always there to support. So I was writing papers in junior and senior year, reading stories, nothing too strenuous.

An honor roll student. I didn't have too much on my mind to deal with. My whole focus was school because I always looked at—I'm a futuristic kind of person so I would look at the future and how something would benefit me. So if I do good grades now, that will help me out in the long run. I was always making honor roll, getting some kind of award or something and just always really trying.

I had problems with math. It just takes me longer to grasp the concept of what is being taught. Sometimes I need individual attention so [the teacher] can really break it down to me so I really see it. I need to see step by step by step kind of thing. Don't skip anything because I'm lost. But math was a little struggle, but once I got it, I was okay with it.

And my English teacher in high school, Mr. Moravian, who was kind of odd because he was in high school with my oldest brother. So it was kind of like, "You were in high school with my older brother and now you're teaching me." I'm like a sister, so it's kind of odd. But from the gate, he could tell what kind of person I was, and he saw what were my strengths and what were my weaknesses. He would always joke with me, but he would always tell me, "Alright, this is what you've got to do," and was always there if I needed help or anything. And I still communicate with him when I go back to high school. I say, "Hey, what's going on?" He's like, "Yeah, we're doing." So we're still cool. He was also my coach for track for two years, so we kind of have a bond, him and I. I emailed him freshman year at Carver just to say, "Hey, what's up? I'm doing good." Just a little check up because I feel like you never know who could help you in the long run, so I just like to keep in contact with people.

Junior and senior year, I was a student leader called an STS leader. And it was a group of upperclassmen who welcomed the freshman and the incoming freshman. We would meet them, we would do freshman orientation, and we would meet with them once a month to see how their classes are going and were there any difficulties like that.

I was part of the Future Educators of America club, so talking about things like why I want to be a teacher, what do you think you can improve, stuff like that. I was a part of track and field sophomore, junior, and senior year. I threw shot put and discus, and I worked in the summer and my senior year. I was a sales clerk at Marshall's senior year.

Carver University

I don't want to say a geek, but I've always been really into school. So I felt like going to college was a must. I want to further educate myself to be something and somebody in this world, to help other people. So I was like, "Go to college? There was no question about it. That's what I want to do. What else am I going to do at home?" Work and now that there is a recession, it's so much going on. You're not guaranteed a job. I feel like if you go to college, you get a degree and teachers are just so needed out there today. I was like I need to go and do something with myself.

I first heard about Carver through a program at my high school called the Source. They were a counseling group and one lady, she provided a college tour—an HBCU college tour. So we went—I don't remember where it was, a community college around the way. And they had all the HBCUs there. I just picked up an application just to apply for it like, "What the heck? I'll just apply because I knew someone that went here. So let me just apply for that." I got in, and I was like shocked. I was like wow.

Why I decided to go to Carver? That's a story! I actually didn't want to. It was the last school on my list. I'm from Jersey. I love Jersey. I live by the shore. I'm a Jersey girl so I'd rather stay in Jersey. That was important. I was planning on going to Kean University or Montclair State. I applied for William Patterson too. Unfortunately, I didn't get accepted to either one of them. I'm not a test taking person. I think my SAT scores had a lot to do with me not getting into the institutions that I wanted to. And Carver was the first acceptance letter I got. I received a scholarship from my high school called the Galen Scholarship. I had to fly in, I had an interview, and they gave me over $12,000.

So I felt like I couldn't go to community college with $12,000. So I'm going to go to Carver, and I'm going to try it out. If I don't like it, I'll transfer. And I was here, and I did not like it whatsoever. The first couple of months I was crying, "Mom, I want to come home. I don't like it here." Because it was just a very different atmosphere. I'm not used to being around so many African Americans. I was always used to a diverse group of people. So being around all that and just seeing how people acted, I just wasn't in touch with that side of me just yet.

It was very different. But I've learned to stick out situations that I'm uncomfortable with. So just stick it out, you have goals. After awhile, I found a group of friends, and I realized I'm only here for my education. So make the best of it. And I knew that if I transferred to another school, a lot of my credits probably wouldn't transfer over. I didn't want to start all over again, so let me just stay here and work it out. I'm happier now. I got adjusted to it a lot better than I was. But it's school.

I feel like I'm just now getting more into the education department. I'm going to be a junior next year, so I feel now it's okay, now you're getting into education classes because recently I haven't taken but one class. I've been taking the university core classes. But as I get more into the education major, I start to see a lot of people that are in the education department in my classes. You get to see a lot of familiar faces. A lot of people in the education department seem very friendly and like to help and get things together with you. We're always contacting each other. "Oh, so how'd you do on this? Did you take the basic skills exam on that?" And even if I have some different ideas on things, so I'll be in class like, "What did you put for this question?" "I got this"—and I'll say, "how did you get that?" So we'll just reflect on each other's thoughts. But everyone is very friendly. Everyone I've come across seems very friendly.

Teaching Career

I think as I left middle school going to high school, I kind of knew I don't have a passion for anything else as I do for kids and wanting to make a difference. So I think, this is it. I want to teach.

And I feel like Ms. Wannamaker had a big influence on me. She made me a strong individual, and she kept pushing me to strive harder and go harder. I feel she pushed me a lot. And I'm like, she did it, and she changed me. What possibly could I do to change other people? I feel like I could do the same thing.

So I want to go out there, and I want to help kids and I want to make a difference in their lives and be a positive influence and have them make it so every time a teacher who wants to be a positive role model for their friends, their peers, their family. Just make them a really influential person.

My friends and family think it was great that I wanted to be a teacher. It probably really didn't matter what I was planning on doing after college as long as I was going to school and doing something. But as soon as I knew, I had a focus, and they're like, "It's a good idea to be a teacher. Go with it. You need it. The money may not be good, but if that's what you're passionate about, go ahead. Go for it."

I want to make the classroom environment comfortable for all the students so they know they can feel comfortable to talk to me and come with their strengths and weaknesses in the classroom and to have their problems outside. I just want to be there for them. They may not have anyone to turn to, and they take their troubles out in school. But I just want to reflect and let it out sometimes, to vent. But I'm going to make sure they understand all the knowledge that's being taught.

If there are any questions, I'm there after school to support you. Just any problems, bullying, we can solve that. Just make it very easy to talk to. I want them to see me as a teacher, but also as a friend who they can tell and confide in.

In my future classroom, teaching and learning will have a variety of things. You know how kids learn different ways? I'm a visual learner so I like to see pictures and stuff like that. But I have to realize people don't learn like that unless you go to auditory learners who they don't mind lecturing and taking notes or mind watching a movie.

I might have hands-on activities too, so you'll know this is how you do it, to deconstruct something and build so they know different ways to learn and kind of strengthen other ways to learn. So if they're a visual learner, think outside your box and try to listen. It may be a little hard at first, but try to give it a go. Just make it a fun environment and have their input on things they would like to do. Not only am I important in the classroom, but we're in this classroom for a reason. I'm here to teach and you're here to learn. So let me know any input you would like to have within the classroom as well.

I know everyone's not perfect. So I may come across a lot of troubled students that may give me a run for my money. But I hope I can support them, and they do a 360 to change them. And I know there are going to be students who are always going to be on task and always doing what they're supposed to do. So I hope to keep that relationship with them and to just welcome them and make sure they're on the right track, no roadblocks, don't let anything get in their way and tell them different.

As for my colleagues, through being so close with my fifth-grade teacher, I've seen the difference of opinions that teachers may have and, "Oh, you shouldn't do that for that lesson plan and that's not a good idea." So I feel like there may be some conflict in ideas. But then there are also people that are like, "Oh, let's work together. Let's have our classes like Jeopardy, against each other." So some ideas may work with each other, some ideas may not.

But at the end of the day, you're there for yourself so you can take the input and think about it. But you can't always just grab it and think they're right. There may be some colleagues I may get along with and may not. But you've got to do what I have to do, so I feel like that's my classroom because I'm teaching that class. I know how they learn and what they like and what they don't like.

As for me, I don't want to be a pessimist, but I feel parents, there will be negative vibes because, of course, every parent thinks their child is good at this and that. But teachers are with their child most of the day. So they know what they're doing and what they're not doing. We can't speak for what happens at home. But in the classroom, they may be disruptive in class and may not be doing their work. So when it comes to a parent teacher conference,

I would let the parent know this is what's happening in the classroom, they might think that's not my child. They're good at home.

And I'd be like, there's another thing coming. Sometimes their child is very different at home than she does now. Some parents are understanding and will take what I would say into consideration. But yeah, just talk to the student and the student will let them know, "Yeah, I've been misbehaving." So it varies. It varies depending on the parent because some parents don't have good thought process. They think their child is, "Oh, this is the perfect child. He doesn't do this to me at home so why would he do that to you at school? I don't believe it." In denial.

After graduation, I'll probably go back home and have a little side job just to get some extra money and get my own apartment. Because most of my outside scholarships, I have to teach for three years after I graduate. If I do not, then I have to give all the money they gave me through these four years back. So go into the classroom as soon as I can. It really doesn't even matter where I teach, as long as I'm in a classroom.

I'd prefer to teach in Jersey. Time may change, time tells what happens. But I'd go to Jersey, anywhere in Jersey, you know. I'd like to teach fourth grade. I feel like it's just the beginning of the learning stage. Of course, you learn stuff, but I feel between third and fifth you're really starting to learn multiplication facts. That's when the learning really begins.

I feel when you're a younger student, you remember stuff a lot more. Because I remember things from fifth grade that Ms. Wannamaker taught me. And it surprised me. She really must have taught us very well if I still remember like, we were learning the body parts one day. We made up a song so it was like the Elvis Presley hipbone, and I remember that. So I feel if you make learning fun then—don't kind of drag it out—some stuff is always going to be useful. You're always going to use your multiplication facts. You're always going to learn how to use your body. So it's kind of helpful.

Five years out, I'm still teaching. I'm going strong. Grad school might be a thought right about now. If I went to grad school, maybe I'd go to be administration, to be a principal or superintendent or something or a counselor, to be a guidance counselor or something like that. At this point in my life, I'm living on my own. I may have a little side job I work for one or two nights of the week just to get some extra money on the side. I'm living a young life. I'm going out, you know? So I'm teaching in a classroom. I'd be able to float. I won't float for them at first, but if they need me for another grade level then we'll work with that. We'll go with that. But not too much different I would think.

Ten years after graduation? Gees. I'm done. I went to grad school and I'm done. I feel like I have the option to be in the school district and play whatever role I want to play. If I want to be a principal, I can be a principal. If I want to be a vice principal or be the guidance counselor, yeah. I'm living a good life. I'm hoping the money has increased by then so that things would be good. Should be stable. I'm married, and I've moved into my own home. Me and my husband are happily married. He owns his own business.

Twenty years, I'm helping develop the curriculum for the grade levels and stuff like that, having input into that. I'm in administration still. I don't always see myself in the classroom. There is always time. There is always room for change and to be different.

****

Jessica worked hard at Carver and maintained a very good and stable GPA. But, like many of the Education Majors, Jessica had a hard time passing the basic skills exam. She, like others, was grandfathered in to graduate with her degree without certification. Yet, this setback did not deter her. The basic skills exam is mandatory in the state for certification, but it is not mandatory in her home state.

So, the following semester after graduation, Jessica followed me to my current institution in New Jersey. There, she took a capstone course with me and completed her student teaching under my supervision. Unfortunately, the student teaching experience was not the best. She had a wonderful cooperating teacher, originally from the Caribbean, who saw Jessica as a daughter. Her cooperating teacher desperately wanted Jessica to succeed as another Black teacher, which meant that the cooperating teacher put extra pressure on Jessica—and Jessica started to doubt her skills.

Although quite successful in her student teaching experience, and after passing the state of New Jersey's teaching exam, she still did not feel ready for the classroom. Jessica started working at a daycare center near her home for a year. Now, she has moved on to substituting with the hopes of getting her own classroom. Jessica stated in an email:

> It [the day care] wasn't the age I wanted to work with. I didn't feel like I was learning a lot, so I made an executive decision to leave and go back to subbing. In the meantime, I have been filling out apps to be on some local public schools in my county. I have also signed up with the subbing company. They help get you subbing jobs and likely to lead into permanent jobs. But, I still have the desire to teach. I'm ready to get back into the public school for the experience and learn new things. I have had great teachers, and I just wanna continue the journey and change lives to build positive people.

Tyrone

"That's it, Tyrone. I am making your laugh my ringtone."[15] *I would often tell Tyrone this when I heard him laughing in the department, as his wonderful and contagious laugh would also have me giggling. But, Tyrone's infectious laugh was often unexpected. He is quite tall and has a certain air of confidence when he enters the room. At first, people find Tyrone hard to read. He can be stoic, sarcastic, and rarely smiles. But quickly people find out that Tyrone is caring, severely intelligent, and extremely loyal. He may not smile when he laughs, but he laughs from his soul.*

Tyrone, raised in Philadelphia, was a Secondary Education, English major, and he was a student that was often the face of the Education Department. He was in the offices helping other students (whether with tutoring, guidance, and the like) and definitely seen as a leader among his peers and friends. Moreover, he was also a formal student leader assisting incoming freshman and also mentored in Boys to Men. He even dedicated his time to mentorship in the summer months. Tyrone would spend the summers at Carver University working in the Upward Bound program. This is a program, sponsored by the U.S. government, to prepare local high school students for college. His journey to being a teacher started with a denial for his calling to the field.

Home

It's my mom, my four brothers and my sister. I'm number four—I have one younger brother and my sister is younger. I was born in Allentown, but I always lived in Philly. We moved when I was really, really young. Before I could walk. My oldest brother is four years older than me, so he was probably in Allentown since he was four. So we're all from Philly. My grandmother—she lives in Philadelphia and then my mom moved and then she came back to Philadelphia. We actually came to live with my grandma. My mom had her problems. I'll just put it that way. My mom, she was always around, but she never really did anything as far as raising us. I feel that we just live together as far as my school or anything because we just live together.

My grandma raised us by herself. My grandma was at work when my mom was out, so she never got remarried after that. She was always by herself raising her kids and then raising us kids. She raised all of us with the exception of my little sister and my younger brother, who she just got—we all lived in foster care for a point. I probably came out of the system when I was probably about three years old. But my younger brother just got out when he was nine years old. So from there, he moved with my aunt. So he doesn't live with me.

My grandma always raised us until she got sick when I was 15. Then when she got sick, I started living with my mom. I was in Logan [section of the city of Philadelphia] for about a year or two years, and now I've lived in Frankford ever since; probably since my sophomore year here. We just moved there not too long ago. My grandma, she's okay now, but they put her in a nursing home. She can still talk. She can walk. You know, she's not that happy.

My dad—I just met him when I was 19, so I don't know what his problem is. I only met him twice. A lot of my cousins live in Allentown, which is where my dad is from. He also lives in Allentown. I'm the one who left. So my cousin was having a house warming and my mom just called him and he showed up. I really didn't care, I guess. My mom wanted me to meet him so bad. Then he started talking about how he wanted to be a part of my life, blah, blah, blah. He was always saying he was gonna do something, but he didn't do it.

And over summer break, when I worked for Upward Bound, we had off Fourth of July and he wanted me to come down to Allentown and meet the rest of the family. He was supposed to come and pick me up. My uncle always comes, picks me up, and takes me back to school. My mom's sister's husband. He always picks me up and takes me back to school. So I didn't have him come get me. So my dad was supposed to come to pick me up, but he never came. He had his mom call me and say, "Well, he's not coming because of whatever, can you get there on your own." And I said, "No." They were like, "Well, try your best" and I was like, "Okay," and then she hung up. I haven't spoken to them since. I was like, okay, they obviously weren't worried about me so I never talked to them again after that—that would be my last time. Because I don't feel like dealing with that. I'm not talking to him anymore, so that's with him.

My grandmother didn't go to college. I'm not sure if she graduated high school. My mom didn't graduate from high school. I think she went and got her GED some years ago, but she never went any further than that. My grandma didn't really check our grades or things like that. She was the type of person like, "You know what to do then just go ahead and do it or don't do it." She had a lot of things to do, and I chose school and my brother chose not to go to school. My brother dropped out in ninth grade in high school, and my other brother dropped out his 10th-grade year, my other brother finished high school and went to community college and I finished, and I'm in college.

My brother's in community, but he enrolled after I did, so I'm still the first to go to college [*laughter*]. It's like, "I still beat you." He graduated high school before I did, but he did City Year[16] instead of going to college. So I enrolled before he did, and he's half into community and half out. He takes maybe a couple credits a year. He's not really sure what he wants to do. He's majoring in education, and he's a psychology minor. He has the same major I do, but he's not really into it as he should be. He just floats around. So we all did our own thing. She would talk to us and tell us what was right about it, but as far as forcing us about school, my grandma never did.

K–12 Educational Experiences

For elementary, I went to a public school called Nickelton. I went there for kindergarten, and then I moved to Warminster. I went to a boarding school called Place of Jesus Christian School. My grandma sent us there for about four years. So from kindergarten to third grade I was there, at Place of Jesus Christian School. I lived and went there.

Boarding school, it made me racist because they were racist. I think we ran into some good people there and some bad people there. We had what are called dorm parents—I call them my aunts and uncles. The people, like the dorm parents, often had their own kids at the time. But the people who we lived with before, they had their own kids and a lot of people that worked there are White and then they have their kids who are White too. And then you'd have the kids who actually go to the school, but most of them are Black though. Some of the dorm parents' kids went there and we went there too, together. The racism came from them and their kids. That was my first exposure to racism. It's something I knew since kindergarten because everybody else in my neighborhood is Black.

My first dorm parents, we did like them and we don't talk to them anymore, but our second ones we still keep in touch with today. We still go over to their house sometimes. They're doing well; they have two kids now, Bobby is the pastor of a church, I forget where he lives, but he lives right outside Philadelphia though. So we still go there. It's not often since I'm in college, but we still go and we still call and stuff. And he wants to marry us at our wedding, so we still have a good relationship with them. So some good things did come out of Place of Jesus and some bad things too.

My most positive influence during my schooling would have to be my third-grade teacher, who's name was Mrs. Tyson. She treated us really well—she really cared about her class. I had Mrs. Ellman, who was my second-grade teacher, and I had Mrs. MacNaughton for my first grade. I remember all of them. I don't know why. Mrs. Ellman and Mrs. Tyson, they really worked well with the kids, and I still remember some of the things we did, crafty things like that.

I left Place of Jesus and came back. The day I came back, I moved with my mom, so the following year I lived in Harrisburg and went to a school called Williamson. But I did only the first semester of my fourth-grade year and then I came back to Nickelton, so that was fourth grade and fifth grade. It was after that, I had moved in with my grandma. Nickelton was all Black—mostly. WAY back in the day—well, I don't remember anybody else there not being Black. Maybe a couple people might have been Spanish, but most of us were Black.

Then, I went to Taylor, which is now a Military Academy, but it used to be a public middle school. Then I went to Malcolm X High School. I graduated in 2006. At first, I liked Malcolm X 'cause I could walk. That's the only reason I went to Malcolm X 'cause I was too lazy to catch the bus, so I didn't apply to Center.[17] I could have gotten in. I didn't want to catch the bus. I didn't think we could afford it. My grandma didn't have money for us to catch the bus. I didn't know that they are giving bus passes for free. I thought, it was gonna cost me money, and I was like, "I know grandma's not gonna have money for that." So I didn't even bother applying to Center. So I just went to the neighborhood school. Because I ended up moving anyway.

So my junior year and senior year, I had to catch the bus there anyway. It was like a train ride and a bus. But SEPTA[18] had gone on strike. So I get up every morning around 5 o'clock and walked to school. It took me like an hour and a half to walk to school every morning. By then, I was living with my mom and she still the same way; she don't care if I go to school as long as I've got a job that's all she cares about. Basically, by then I had decided that I was gonna do the school thing. I was in 11th grade, I had a lot of friends, I had teachers who had high expectations working in the school, not outside, and I had said to myself—I didn't want to sit out of school 'cause God knows how long SEPTA's gonna be on strike, so I decided to walk. The strike lasted about three weeks.

There was Mrs. Hatfield, who was in the 11th grade; she was a really good English teacher, to the point where she got me through my 12th-grade year. My English teacher was really good because she got me through my senior year. I did work really hard on my senior project. It was a 12-page paper on the Patriot Act. Now that's boring.

My social studies teacher, who was also influential, Mr. Mandelin, he helped me come up with that project because it had to be something educational—it couldn't be simple—so the Patriot Act, he was like you should do that, this is happening and that's happening with the Patriot Act. It sounded interesting at first, but it wasn't. I had to do the paper anyway. I decided that what I was going to do. I knew everything that I knew how to do; it was 12 pages, I had put little political cartoons in it that went with the theme of whatever I was doing. And I worked really hard on it.

And then my 12th-grade English teacher, Ms. Stern, looked through it, she was like—she really just thumbed through it and was like, "Oh, I think you could do better." And she gave me a B. And I had another student who actually just graduated from Carver this semester, he had just copied some things from the Internet and you could still see the URLs and stuff—and she didn't look at his paper either, but she gave him an A.

But, Mrs. Hatfield, she expected a lot of you. She was hard too. Actually I was in an Honors English course, but they didn't tell you. Don't ask why. They tell you after you do the class because they didn't want people to feel bad or to feel like you're better than the other people.

Mrs. Hatfield used to talk about success. I used to think you're not successful if you're gonna be a teacher. Oddly, I'm studying to be a teacher now, but I wasn't at the time. So she was talking about how she came from the Philippines. She was talking about coming from her country and making it over here and going through college and everything. She had a master's degree in education—and she was just a really good teacher. Stuff that she did also I still remember—and that's why I think it makes a good teacher, when you can remember it years later some of the stuff they did. The things she taught us, it had actually gotten through senior year and to college.

My 12th-grade teacher taught nothing; Ms. Stern worked on the same Shakespeare thing all year long, and all she did was talk about how educated she was, how she got this degree and that degree, but she never did anything actually. She never collected any work, and she lost my journal book. It was really bad. She was in her 50s, and she had been teaching for like 30 years, ruining kids year after year I bet [laughter]. All she talked about was how many years she had left before she could retire. She didn't do anything. And all she did was sit there at her desk and, "All right, we're gonna do this today," and if you didn't do it, she would be sitting there—"All right, we're gonna take a quiz now." So I tried to make the class fun by reading Shakespeare in character, but it was usually little stuff like that, but then I was like, "Okay, I'm done with this." So I stopped going to class.

I took regular English my senior year. I took AP statistics, and I was like, "I don't want to take two AP classes. I might fail." So I took regular English and that's because I was already into English, so there was no need to take it extra, so I took regular English. If I took AP English with the other teacher, who most of my friends took it with, and she challenged them and they did learn. And we didn't learn or read anything.

Most of my schooling was teacher-centered, so I learned that way. That was someone teaches it, and then I applied it myself, then I learn how to do it. So the teacher-centered didn't really do too much. I had a few teachers who did student-centered things—teachers who would read to us from the textbook that got us to start reading on our own and things like that. But most of the instruction I had was teacher-centered.

It varied by year, but usually I did pretty well, and I never struggled in school. The variation would be sometimes I felt like doing the work and sometimes I didn't feel like doing it. But it was never a struggle to me being in school, though. But like I said, my grandma never enforced it, so it was my own willpower. I feel like going then alright, I feel like it, or nah, I don't feel like doing it.

I was never involved in anything extracurricular until maybe my senior year of high school. I was in the National Honor Society. Also, I did Dwayne Smith, which is like a competition. You've gotta come up with a problem in your neighborhood and your team from your school would figure out how to solve that problem. And your team from your school will sit around and solve that problem, and then you present at the National Constitution Center in front of the mayor who was supposed to come and actually didn't come, and the governor who was supposed to come but actually didn't come. But it was a pretty good time. And basically it was Malcolm X and four other local charter and private schools. But our team was the only public school, and we won that year. But the money that we were supposed to get for our project didn't come till late and by then we were all seniors and you know how seniors die out—they didn't feel like doing it anymore. So we actually never got our project started, which was a good project.

So after that, I started getting involved by doing student government, and I became a senior resident, which is an internship where you shadow a teacher or another worker within the school—kind of like the Junior Year Practicum[19] at Carver. Just like that. I followed the Dean's secretary. She would do office work, so I would learn office skills, teaching me stuff like that. How to use one of those big copiers and all that other stuff.

Carver University

Some people called Fundamentals[20] took over Malcolm X. I know a lot of them too and since I was involved in the project, they paid people to be an intern. So they were like, "So hey, um, Tyrone, which college are you going to?" And I was like, "None." They were like, "What?!" So they went off, and I got vouchers for the application fees and they would mail them for me. So the only thing I had to do was just fill out the application.

I applied to a lot of schools, and I got into all of them accept Chestnut Hill. They wanted another letter of recommendation, which I got. But by the time they sent me that, I had already got accepted to seven schools. So I thought, "Do I want to really be there?" but there was no point. So Chestnut Hill came off the list. About half the schools I applied for as an English major and the other as a business major. Like Penn State, I did English, Carver I did business. I think Chestnut Hill College, I did education. I think IUP, I did business. I didn't know which one, so I just did every other one. That's because I didn't know what I wanted to do.

I didn't actually pick Carver. You know that rolling admissions thing going on. Okay, Penn State I couldn't afford. I can't afford anything, but I started to think about what's the one I want to be at. IUP is much cheaper, and it's an in-state schools. I mean it was even cheaper than Carver actually. So I thought I would go to IUP and most of my friends were going there, you know you want to party in college with your friends.

I only applied to Carver because of Ms. Cannon, she's one of those bad teachers I had, she was having one of her terrible days of teaching and the people from Carver came that day. So they came to join that class so I could get out of that class and not be there for her to teach. And I would do anything to get out of her class. Even go see the Carver people, and I heard a lot of bad things about Carver. People would say, it's a party school, it's a dirty school, it's violent. This thing happened to that person, that thing happened to that person, higher age population, blah, blah blah. And all you heard was bad about Carver, so I went and was like, "See you later, Ms. Cannon. I'm gonna be at this thing."

So I went, and they gave us an application and a tour. And I sent out the rest of the information. I figured I might as well go ahead and send one out for

Carver too since it was free since Fundamentals was going to send it out for me anyway. So I sent it out and got accepted. IUP called me during the summer, so I was supposed to go up there for testing and all that. You know IUP is about 6 hours from Philadelphia to drive. I wasn't gonna go because nobody was gonna drive me, and it would have been 8 hours on the bus.

IUP sent me a letter saying that they had run out of housing for students and that I could enroll, but I would have to live off campus. And I was looking at apartment living guides to find an apartment out there. I was like, "Okay, I'm working with no money here." I'm going out here with what they call a dollar and a dream, so the idea of me going all the way down to IUP to look for another place to live was probably not gonna happen. I was like, I have to do something else. I didn't tell my mom because I didn't have anybody to help me pick out schools, so I didn't know which schools were good schools and which schools were bad schools. So I didn't hear until afterwards which schools were the good schools, and the schools I got accepted to and didn't go because I didn't know if they were good schools or not. I just went with anything.

But Carver, at that time, they had with the acceptance that we need to hear from you by this time or you're not accepted. At that time it had been late summer. Late, late summer, and it was almost time for school when I heard from IUP and Carver was the only school that was still letting people come at that time. And so that's why I came. I would do anything to leave—I didn't want to be home anymore. Me and my mom were not getting along at all anyway. We get along much better now that I'm not home. But at the time, I couldn't understand her and she didn't understand me, I couldn't stand her boyfriend. He actually liked me, but I didn't like him. So I was like, "Okay, I'm gonna go to Carver because I'm going to school. I don't care where I go." So when I heard back from Carver, I just thought I'll make the best of it.

I was planning to transfer, but I actually stayed because I loved it. I fit in, you know. Carver has a great history, it had a lot of great things going on, it was just some people here made it look bad here for everybody. And that's Carver's problem, that's our only problem.

I wanted to try something new. Basically, I came to Carver, and I just wanted to be different in college than I was in high school. As far as being involved and doing what I need to do. First thing I did was join the Gospel choir, then from there I decided to do more.

Honestly, I didn't know what to expect of the Education Department. I didn't know what it took to be a teacher. What it did for me was give me respect for the teachers I had that were good teachers because the major has a lot of requirements. As far as the teachers, the education professors I met, I've enjoyed everyone I've had so far. I know what I have to do. I know the requirements. It's a lot more than I expected—a lot, a lot more. Even from taking Introduction to Education, it's a lot more than I expected. The people are fun, it's just what I was meant to do. Even when I do struggle, I started the class like, "Oh God, this class is gonna be so hard." Even from the start, I was like, "Oh goodness, I don't know about this class." I got through so well because it was what I was supposed to do, so it just happened. So I just take it year by year.

Teaching Career

I actually always wanted to teach, and I don't know what made me, but I never thought about it until I got here at Carver. For me, I think when I got here—I've only took one course in Business which was Finite Math, so I didn't like it at all. The idea of being a business major I didn't like. I took Introduction to Education as a core course. I did really well in the class. I knew that was what I was supposed to be doing.

You know when you're supposed to do something, but you just don't want to do it? Like, you don't want to listen. I didn't want to be an Education major because I didn't want to be broke; we were always broke—always. And people are always talking about how, even teachers themselves, they were complaining and they were always going on strike. Teachers were terrible in my classroom, most of them were. Most of them had no motivation. They were there because they were getting paid badly. Every teacher I had complained, with the exception of one, Ms. Hatfield.

I've always known people for being like the brokest people ever, and then the major was really hard and it wasn't really worth it at all. That's what made me say, "Okay, I'm going into business." I'm the kind of person that is adaptable. I adapt to anything; I thought I could be in the business world just fine, and I would make it just fine—that's the kind of person I am. But I knew what I was supposed to do, but I didn't do it. I just gave that up and said, "Alright, let me just go ahead and do what I'm supposed to do."

I probably wouldn't have been happy at Carver taking all these business courses. If I stayed with all these business courses, I probably struggled my way through. You have the struggle that it takes to learn, but you don't have the passion behind it. I don't have the passion for business, so the struggle is gonna be there regardless, but the passion pushes you the rest of the way. So I was like, "Okay, let me go ahead and go through with everything else." So I took Introduction to Education to see if that's what I really wanted to do, and I was like, "Yeah this is it."

Actually, I hadn't told my mom up until the last year that I switched my major from business, and my uncle just found out, the one that takes me up here, and he's always like, "Yeah, when you're in Business, your gonna do this and do that," and I just let him talk. I never told him that I'm in Education up until now. So he's like, "What's happening? You want to be a teacher?" And I was like, "Yeah." "Really?" And I was like, "Yeah." And he just looked blank, and I was like, "Whatever." I spoke to him about why I wanted to do this, but all they think about is money. I told him, "Well, in Business they have outsourcing going on and all that stuff, so I would be in the Business world with no job, a degree with no job, trying to do whatever I can do and I probably wouldn't work in the field because of what's going on right now in the economy. Education is more and whatever is going on, they're not gonna look for teachers out of the country." So he's like, "Oh yeah, oh yeah." I mean, he supports me whatever I do because I'm the only one who's only ever gone to college anywhere. The only person in my family from my grandma down who ever went to college is my aunt, but that's it.

My brothers don't really care about what major I'm in—it's just college work to them. So they have the notion like, "Don't you know this? You're in college. Don't you know that? You're in college. Don't you know everything?" like God came down and placed everything in your brain once you went to college. You know, I have to be a Mr. Know-it-all. But they never really ask me much about my major. They are like, "You want to be a teacher by then, okay."

I decided to teach English because of the good teachers I had talked about like Ms. Hatfield and there's a few others. And the bad teachers, which is what I see more of—the teachers who teach English and teach it poorly. Oftentimes, a lot of college students come here and don't even have the skills and what they need to be in college. And that's what I feel that happens in high school. So I decided to teach English and my goal is for me to give something better so when they be extremely challenged, overly challenged, and I'm the teacher nobody likes because they're so challenged. But when they leave, they'll appreciate the fact that they have all the skills that are necessary to go in college and can graduate in four years because they don't have to take this class and that class and catch up to where they're supposed to be in high school.

My goal is to start that movement within my school and within my district and within the state, and so on. And also I want to come up with my own theory—that's why I'm gonna get a doctorate—I want to know what really works. I want to try it by trial and error.

This whole problem with the achievement gap and all this stuff, I'm tired of talking about it and trying to see if we can realize it. I want to actually contribute and be a major part in fixing it. And not just exposing the gaps with numbers and records, but to actually help people be educated and people to actually really do something and for people to be proud of what they've done and to go to college and become what they want to become because they've had the background to do whatever. That's pretty much my goal for teaching. Also, I want to teach at the college level. I want to train people to do it right, so I want to work from both sides.

Like I said before, I had a mixture of teachers that are classroom-centered, so—and knowing that people learning differently. I was somehow versatile in learning—teacher-centered class and student-centered. I know a lot of kids aren't. I think it comes from being schooled in different environments like I was. I went from the private school to the public school, so I think I had a wider range of things, which is why I was able to move through whatever the teacher was doing for that year, but a lot of students can't do that. They've always been strictly in one environment. So my classroom would look more like my educational experience, which is, first of all, I'd do a lot of teacher-centered stuff, but then I will switch it up with a lot of student-centered stuff. If I could think of my ideal classroom, it would be a perfect mixture of both. They can hear what I need to say, but also they can apply it themselves. When I learned, you can talk and talk and talk, but if I don't apply it, I won't remember it. I can't just listen and be okay with it. I must do something with myself in order to learn it. That's the only way I can do it. So I want to have a mixture of both of them.

As far as students, I hope to be that teacher that a few would talk about how they still keep in contact with me and invite me to their wedding, they did this, they did that. All this stuff because they were a big influence, or I was a part of their lives. I hope to give back. Outside of school, I hope to do the mentoring thing. I mentor for myself, and I mentor for others. I want that relationship where you can go to your teacher for not only help with homework, but if you're having trouble at home and that person can come to you. I know as a teacher that there are certain things that you're not allowed to do based on the school district, but the person who you come to and they can go to you for help so you can lead them where they need to go so they can have that person. I know a few teachers who used to do it, and then things got out of control with the law, and teachers had to be more separated from their students in classrooms. But, at least, I want to be that influential person that can open the gate and help you get to where you need to go and always be a part of that person's life.

I also hope to educate parents. As far as my parents, my grandma and my mom, who have never been involved in school, I hope to get parents more involved because there are certain aspects of school where you need, or at least you want, parents to be there. Like when you have award ceremonies or you've done well or you want somebody to be there to say you've done well. I hope that I can be that teacher that can influence parents to be more involved in their school.

Education starts at home, and then there's a lot of things that parents need to do in order for education to work properly. I just hope to build a relationship not only with the students, but with the parents, so we're a team working for the better of this child. I need your help and you need my help, and we need to do it together. I'm not any better than you, I don't care what background you have, I don't care if you've never been educated, I don't care if you dropped out in third grade—your child needs you, and I need you so we can do this thing right. You want something better for your child, and I want something better for your child, so let's work together.

I want to do what a lot of people and teachers I've seen do which is teach and go to graduate school at the same time. My first year, or hopefully by my second year. And then after that I want to go straight through with my degrees. I want to be able to teach while working on my degrees in education. I want to use my degree in education to do whatever it is that I do as far as all the other stuff I talked about and teach. Eventually, I don't know after how many years, move to the college level. I'm not really sure how fast I want to make that transition or if I will—I might like high school enough to stay. I definitely want to work in administration though. So I might move on to college after like maybe 20 years. I'm not exactly sure how I'm going to make the transition, but I know I want to do it. I know I want to do it. My career is basically just schooling and teaching and figuring out the path I decide.

I want to probably be in the Philadelphia school district. If I want to extend my horizons too, so I might be in a district similar like Elizabeth, New Jersey or like maybe somewhere in New York or maybe in Baltimore or somewhere like that—I'm not sure. But I do want to be in the areas where there are people like me who don't have what I have—I always had the feeling that I could do better than what was going on, so no matter what, I was sticking with school. And a lot of people, they don't have that. Because there were no mentors, there were not influential people, there was none of that. All there was was you, and then all the people who were just like you were people who were dropping out of school and people who were doing what they wanted to do, people who were making a lot of money doing other things without going to school and you're stuck in school—you start looking at that instant gratification and you wonder, "I want that too, so I'm gonna get out of here." But for some reason, I always knew that I needed to stick with school, so I always did. But I know a lot of people who didn't do that. So I want to be in those areas where you can influence the people who aren't like me, who don't have the, "Okay, I'm gonna do this no matter what" feeling and get them to the college level. So I want to work where I grew up—the public school.

I would like to teach in urban areas, but I want to expand my horizons. I don't want to just stick with everything I've done. I want to go through the other kind of schools where there's one Black kid there and things like that. Because I know I'm working for Upward Bound and a lot of those kids are like that, and they need people like me just as badly. So I'm not exactly sure how I'm gonna go about it. I wish I could be everywhere at once kind of.

Ten years after graduation, I'll probably just be teaching. By now, I will have done all I can do education-wise, so I'll be using that to make my teaching better and to look at myself and evaluate myself to see where I'm most effective, see where I lack and improve and continue to build up that research of what works and what doesn't work. Actually, I want to write a book. I'll start that capacity in my life. I have started writing a book already.

Twenty years, I'll probably still be in a high school environment, but I probably will be in the midst of transitioning into the college level. I plan on being in the high school for a while—I know that—but I just know I want to do college as well.

****

Tyrone completed all the certification requirements and student teaching successfully. At student teaching, he still was unsure if he should teach in an urban area or be a role model for those few students in the rural classroom. He decided to do his student teaching in a rural setting, but unfortunately, he and another student teacher in the same school came across racist and unfair treatment from the administration. This confirmed his decision to stay and teach in an urban area.

After graduation, Tyrone went back to Philadelphia and worked as an after-school Program Assistant at a public high school. The following year, he signed on at a charter school to be an eighth-grade language arts teacher. He remained there for three years and also became the head of the English department and Team Leader within one year's time of working at the school. After those three years, Tyrone moved to another charter school within the area teaching ninth- and 10th-grade English.

Tyrone continued his dream with higher education, and two years after graduating from Carver, he started working on his MEd at a major institution in Philadelphia. Not liking the program, Tyrone left it and began the following year at another institution in the city. He is still currently working on his MEd in Special Education while teaching.

· 5 ·

JUNIOR YEAR: PRACTICING TEACHER

Shironda

Shironda is a small and gorgeous woman with a personality and dynamic that gets people's attention. I first met Shironda when she was a senior in high school through a non-profit organization on which I sat on the Board. She came to interview for a scholarship for high schoolers planning to major in education. In the interview, Shironda came with a very low GPA (2.0 range) from high school, but she explained how she "got her act together" late in her high school career, and she was determined to be an excellent teacher. Shironda promised, "I won't let you down."

Behind closed doors, there was a real debate if we should give Shironda this competitive scholarship, as she just did not have the grades. But I and one other person knew that there was just "something" about this woman. Shironda got the scholarship, and she actually chose to come to Carver University as a Secondary Education, English major.

Shironda did not hold back, and she kept her promise. From freshman year, she was voted in as class president and kept her seat through most of her college career. Also, she maintained a high GPA and was the president of Kappa Delta Pi—the education major's honor society—and president of the Education Club. I left Carver University Shironda's sophomore year, but I came back to co-teach an intensive urban course with a colleague, and I was fortunate to have Shironda as a student then. Shironda's story of wanting to be a teacher in her home of Philadelphia was long and winding.

Home

A majority of my family is African American. My mom and dad—well, my biological mom and dad, they're both on drugs—crack. My parents are still on drugs. But I grew up with my grandfather. I always was with my grandpops since I was one. So he raised me. The majority of the time growing up, it was all boys. I lived in a house with all boys growing up—me and my three brothers. I'm the first girl, second child on my mom's side, but on my dad's side I'm the last girl out of six kids, last child.

I always lived with my grandpop, but my mom has always been in and out of my life. I didn't meet my dad until I was in the ninth grade, and that's when I got introduced to the rest of my brothers and sisters on my dad's side. But on my mom's side, I always knew her side of the family and then my grandpop's side of the family. But he's not my biological grandfather, but he's my brothers'.

My grandpop, he did a great job of taking care of me and my brothers. So my gram died when I was 6. But at the same time, it was always you've got to fend for yourself because you're the only girl. So it wasn't that I was left out, but he just put me on a high pedestal. When I was 12, I learned how to cook the whole Thanksgiving dinner. I prepared breakfast, lunch, and dinner for the household. When I was 13, he put me on his bank account so I paid the bills. So I was dealing with probably over $1,500 a month and I had to pick okay, "Shironda, are you going to go spend your money with your girlfriends or are you going to pay the bills?" So I always had a lot of responsibilities.

My grandpop, he's still living but he don't take care of us no more. And my grandpop, we fine, but I don't really talk to my grandpop right now because of family situations. But, I take care of my younger brother. I come home on the weekends to check on him and since I became his caregiver, but it's not under the court, it's kind of frustrating. Because since he was 18 and I'm 19, they're like, "Well, he's 18, he's grown now." But because of the way my grandpop raised us, he's not the average 18-year-old. So he still needs somebody to you know, check on his homework, make sure he's going to school.

So now I take care of my little brother that comes after me. But my oldest brother, that's the first child on my mom's side, he's just on the streets right now. Like dealing, but he's not on crack or nothing. He's just dealing. He's been on the streets since 11th, 10th grade. He dropped out of high school.

Growing up, my mom was just on the street. She was kind of stable. I remember growing up I still looked at my mom as my role model as a woman. Even though I knew she was doing drugs, it was like she was more stable at one point growing up. Now, today, no, she's not stable. But you know, growing up she was. She still made sure she put cards for us in the mailbox. My grandpop was real big on family, so he would always say, "No matter what, respect your mom." And he would let us go see her. We didn't really probably talk to her too long. She never took anything from me, no money or nothing. So she always was stable until I got to a certain age. Then she started taking money from us when I was around 12.

But my mom, very educated. Went all the way to college, went to Pierce College, got a high school diploma, graduated honors of her class. She never graduated college, though. But then when she got introduced to drugs by my aunt, that's her only sister. So my grandmom had two daughters. It was just my mom and my aunt. So my aunt introduced her to drugs and then when she met our dads, they already was kind of on drugs at that point. So it just made her habit more of a habit.

But my dad, when I got my high school diploma, he just got his—it's not a high school diploma because he went back. He just got his GED at 50 years old, so good for him for going back at 50.

K–12 Educational Experiences

I started off at Greedon Elementary in South Philadelphia. I can say elementary school was probably my second favorite experience. The reason why I liked elementary school is because since I grew up in a house with all boys, Greedon's where I learned to be a young lady at. They had puberty classes there for us and my grandpop didn't know nothing about it. So anything that was for free to keep me at school, I loved school. When I first started school, I loved it so much.

I felt like somebody when I was in school. So, in elementary school, I was so active. I went and did the safety team, and I wanted to stay after school. I wanted to help the teacher. I wanted to be the teacher's helper. And I did everything. So I liked elementary school.

But I guess I didn't like moving on to middle school at all because when I moved on to middle school, I got scared when it was time for sixth grade because I didn't know where I was going to school. You know, everybody else, you get a choice[21] for schools. And my grandpop, we didn't really have a choice at home because growing up, having my grandpop as my caregiver, he didn't know nothing about school choice or anything. It was just wherever they send you next, that's where they send you next.

So I had to end up going to London Middle School, and I remember this is when my mom, she was kind of active, and I told her, I don't want to go there. Everybody in the neighborhood said you get bullied there and it's mean there. And I don't want them to pick on me. And she said my grandma went there, so I'm about to live a legacy. My mom got me all excited, and she showed me my grandma's middle school yearbook. And she was like, "See, you're going to be fine."

And then when I got to school the first day, it was like my grandma couldn't have went there. Like, "No, not this school. This is horrible." The first day kids were getting jumped on their way going to school. So I'm running inside my classroom. Middle school, I didn't like it at all. I didn't want to go to class, and that's where I kind of started to find my true self then because I realized do I really like school. "Is school for me?" That's how I always thought of middle school as, "is school for me or is school not for me," instead of saying this is an education, I'm supposed to get it. Then I started to get picked on by peers at my school. "Oh, your hair is nappy."

And then as I was moving up in the stages of middle school, I started not understanding the curriculum. And the teachers always seemed—I was always loud. That's what I was considered, a loud child in middle school. "You so loud, Shironda. Be quiet. Be quiet." And nobody never took me to the side and was like, "You know, why are you so loud? Why do you do this?" Like, I never had no one ever take me to the side. And I know for a fact not one teacher never took me to the side, never asked why I acted the way I acted. Never asked why my grandpop never came to get my stuff. So I just felt like they didn't care no more.

So when I got to the eighth grade, once again, I wasn't prepared because that's when we're supposed to pick for high school. So they were going to send me to Eastern and so that was my neighborhood high school in South Philadelphia. And I was like, "No Pop, you can't make me this time. Please don't. Please don't." And the neighborhood schools, they didn't have enough room for us in Eastern. So they made London students go up to the ninth grade. And this is when I decided I can't do London either. So I stopped wanting to come to school.

So my grandpop, he was elderly, so by the time then I learned my grandpop's routine, he took a morning ride every morning. I'm like, "Okay, I got to stay in school until 10:00 and then I'm leaving." Then I got to be home by 6:00 because I was supposed to be at my after-school program. I just stopped liking school altogether. I walked out of teachers' classrooms. I told them, "I don't care. You going to fail me, oh well. I don't want to be here no more."

And one thing that I definitely remember is they never told us how important high school was with the credit system. I never knew nothing about that. They didn't say this is ninth grade. This is a start over. So I'm thinking that I got the same grades following me since the sixth grade. So I'm like, "No, I'm already messed up." I already got bad attendance. "No, I don't want to stay in school." So I started skipping school, and I started seeing my little "boyfriend" at that time. And I would go to his house every single day.

When I would skip school, I'd never skip school on Fridays. My Uncle Clark would come get me for church on Friday nights. I had to be home early and sometimes he would stop at the school. So my dearest teacher never understood why I came on Fridays. That's because my uncle was coming to get me. I never skipped Fridays.

So my Uncle Clark, I'll never forget, like if I ever had to pick anyone or the reason why I'm so successful today would be my Uncle Clark. I always brought home the Cs and the Ds and the Fs. And my Uncle Clark would always be like, "It's alright. I started off like that." But with him, it really was. He would take me to get milkshakes like I got the best report card in the whole wide world. We always went to McDonald's and got a milkshake and fries every time I got a report card. He inspired me. When I got to the 10th grade, he had passed away.

Then closer to the end of the school year, the counselor at The Success Center at London, they told me, "Well, Shironda, you got to think of an alternative." I'm like, nobody wants me. I'm tired of going to neighborhood high schools. Nobody wanted me. And he was like, write other neighborhood high schools. I was like, "Okay." So the counselor, he started me from scratch. I wrote to four different schools.

So I started getting acceptance letters. My Uncle Clark that was active in my life, he was like, "I really think you should go to Overhill. It's close. I'll take you your first day," because my grandpop, his sickness or his arthritis started to get bad. So that's when I had decided to go to Overhill.

But, going to Overhill, I had to take a bus and a train and a bus to school. I got up every morning, 6:45 when I wasn't on drum line. But when I was on drum line, I had to be there at 6:45, so I left like 5:00 a.m. So it took about an hour and 45 to two hours to get to school.

Then when I first got there in 10th grade, I didn't want to participate until I met my high school best friend. And I switched it up. When I got there, my uncle—he had told me, "You know, let's start off on a clean slate. You've got to do well." When I first got there, I didn't like it because I didn't know that you had to switch classes. So I'm following the same first class all day. They had me as skipped for the first week. I'm calling my grandpop. I'm like, "I went to class, told the ladies my name. They don't got my name on the roll sheets, and that's because I was in the wrong class."

But from skipping school in the ninth grade and middle school, I was so behind. And my English teacher didn't know because I was good with faking. So I would just act like I knew everything. But I knew how to do the work, but I didn't understand it. I always knew how to write, but I don't know how to write correctly. I'm great with my ideas. I'm great with brainstorming. But my words would be incorrect. I have a lot of misspelled errors, run on sentences. But nobody took out the time to help me.

I would just go to my best friend's house every day after school, told my grandpop it was the homework club. And I would get her to help me with my homework. But of course, you know, when it's your friend, they don't really help you so much. They just say alright, do this or this or copy off of mine. But my strength was math. So I would help her with her math, and then I'd do her math, she'd do my reading. So that's how I really got through high school. I was still getting one F now compared to me having four Fs before. So my uncle, once again, he didn't mind. He was like, "It'll get better, it'll get better."

At home, I was getting frustrated because I'm like, "I'm a girl and I'm tired of being in this house with all boys." But then I told my grandpop, like I'm really unhappy. And he just was like, you do need a woman figure in your life. So my sister on my dad's side, my sister Janie, she took me in the 10th grade. She was 26 or 27 then. When I first started living with her, she was just, "Your grades are the worst," and this is when I really tried. When I got the third report card period, she was like, "This is terrible," and all my teachers were just like, "This is wonderful." Janie was like, "This is not acceptable. I'm not taking this." Like no—and I'm really trying.

And I'll never forget this one lady named Miss Green. This was our academy leader. And she was just telling me I'm so proud of you. And I never had nobody say that to me before. I always had my uncle say you know, "It'll get better, it'll get better." But she was like, "I'm so proud of you. I bet you'll have As and Bs the next report card period." And I was like, "Watch, I am." Because for once somebody gave me a compliment. Even my teachers would say, "Oh well, this is you. This is my paycheck. This is what I do." But with Miss Green, she was like, "Nope." She just said I'm proud of you, that's it. And she was like we can get this next report card period. And the next report card period, I'll never forget, my last marking period, I brought home all passing grades. It wasn't As and Bs, but I didn't have no Ds and no Fs. And she gave me the most improved award.

One day in school, there was an opportunity for a scholarship program for people with Fs on their transcripts. I was like, "I wish I could just throw my report card away." The scholarship woman said, "Well, you can't throw it away. But this is a fresh start. So don't worry about nothing you had in ninth grade, don't worry about nothing you had in 10th grade. Let's worry about 11th grade. And I promise you if you start from 11th grade, you can go to college." So I'm like, "College?" so this is the first time I found out about college, 11th grade. So I was like, "Miss Sammie, what's college?" And you know, she kind of made the face like I didn't know. But I guess after a while she caught on because I wasn't smiling. And she was like, "Okay, I'll show you."

The scholarship program met on Drexel's campus. So she took me outside and she said, "Well, what do that see?" And I said Drexel because I thought I was at a hospital. And she said, "No, this is a college. We're staying in a college building right now." I said, "Why is this classroom set up like this? Why don't they have chairs like us and desks?" And she was like, "Well, in college, you've got to be a little bit more comfortable. You get to be treated like a young adult." Little by little, the more I did better in school, the more she told me about college. So it was like a trade off. You do good in school and you do your homework and bring it to the scholarship program and you show me how you're doing. And she told me to put myself on a daily report. And I never knew I could do that. So she would check my daily reports. And if my daily reports were good, she'd tell me more and more information about college. So then she entered me in a scholarship program to go to Europe. So I was like, "Miss Sammie, they're not going to let me go. I'm not good at writing. I'm not good enough to go to the other side of the world. Where is Europe at anyway?" She was like, "Shironda, you're the most dedicated student I have." Every marking period, first marking period, second marking period, third marking period, all As and Bs. I felt like the president of the United States at the scholarship program because everybody looked up to me and all the teachers and stuff always wanted my help. But of course Miss Sammie didn't know that I was still struggling in reading.

She just knew that I'm a very hard worker and if I want something I'm going to make sure I get it. So I wrote my letter so that I could go to Europe. Out of 500 people in the scholarship program, only five could go and I was one of the five. When I got to 11th grade, that's what they considered me, Overhill's finest because I just turned and did a whole 360. But it was all starting with Miss Green believing in me.

In 12th grade, I applied for a teacher scholarship through the school district. It's $10,000 for four to five years of college if you're going to school to be a future teacher. And I ran against every child that wanted to be a teacher in the actual district, in the Philadelphia school district. And once again—this time it was only three people that could win out of the school district, and I won out of the three people.

Carver University

I love Carver because when I first went on my college tour with the scholarship program in the 11th grade, program in 11th grade and when I went to Carver, I just remember the people that was there that gave us the tour guide when we went. They were still in school and they just said this is your home away from home. That's the quote that they always used. Every single person you ran into that whole entire day, and I mean this is people from night to day. We stayed at Carver the longest because we were waiting for our bus to come back. But at the end of the day, this is my home away from home.

It inspired me. And we went all the way down South Carolina, we went all the way down there. Up in Elizabeth City and all the other schools, Penn State, Temple and I just said I wanted to go to Carver. But Carver denied me. They denied me at first. See, this is why it's about who you know. Because Carver definitely denied me at first. So if you ever Google my name, it says that I go to another HBCU.

So an employee at Carver, Ms. Martin, she found out I wasn't going to Carver because she saw the Google article with my scholarship, they got a national paper that come out. And she said well, "Why does it say you're going to [another HBCU]?" And I'm like, "Ms. Martin, they didn't accept me." And she was like, "No, I'm going to get you another interview. You ready?" And she came to get me the day after my prom, the day after literally. So when everybody else wasn't going to school the day after prom, I was going to Carver. She took me to Carver, she gave me an interview with her.

Then I had an interview with the head lady that's in charge, and then they said I was accepted. So I didn't get accepted to Carver until May.

I tell my friends at other colleges about the support I get from Carver, and sometimes they don't believe me. As a education department, it's no I in TEAM. There are some great faculty. It's people like that that just says you can't do it halfway. You got to come out certified. You can't go half way for your students. Like they make it about more than just me. They say it's not about you not being certified. You really want to be teaching someone and not be highly qualified? Do you really want somebody's parent coming up to you and judging your teaching abilities? And it's just like they help you think outside the box. Taking the easy way out is not always the best route all the time.

And I said if I ever got a chance, I would turn my weakness into my strength. So my weakness is English. Right now, I still think I don't read on my right reading level. But I try every single day. I read more. When I go back to Overhill, I get my teacher to reassess me to see if I'm going up levels and what reading level I am at. Because with her, there's no embarrassment because she exactly knows where I started at. But with some people, like when I'm in college sometimes, I was kind of scared to tell the professors, even though we've got remedial classes at Carver, I don't think they know how remedial I am. Because I could place out of their classes but still need help.

I actually go to the Success Center at Carver, and they help me with pronouncing my words, with you know, increasing my vocabulary and starting over. Making sure I got my parts of speech down pat, making sure I know how to write the correct type of sentences and making sure that I don't write the way I speak.

I love the peers there. Well, I guess because I'm very active since I'm the president of Kappa Delta Pi, the president of the Education Club. And starting off as a freshman, I started off as a secretary of the Education Club. Yes, I was the president of my class but being involved in my career choice and being involved on campus, I kind of put it in two different categories. Like I honor being the president of Kappa Delta Pi and Education Club. It's more of an honor to me than even being the president of the school or SGA, our student government association.

Teaching Career

My primary goal as a teacher is to put more hope into the kids. I want my students to feel like it's never too late. That's my main theme. That's my goal, is it's never too late. But I just want to make sure that whatever I do, I don't want to give up on them. Like no matter what, it can be the child that everybody's like, "No, he's the problem child. He or she is the problem child. You won't be able to do it. You won't be able to do it."

I just want to be the teacher that says I put in the extra work, extra time, whatever it took to get the job done. But I don't want recognition for it because that's when I think it becomes complicated. When you try to do things to impress people, it makes your job harder instead of just doing it because it needs to be done—so that's the type of teacher I want to be.

And I just want my classroom. I want to feel like since I want to teach middle school or high school, I don't want the rewards or stickers or giving them out pencils or making my classroom colorful and stuff. Because they're in middle school or high school because that's when I remember when I got to middle school or high school, the classroom was boring. Everything was black and white. You didn't get a pencil no more, they didn't put stickers on our papers—they said you're too old for that. You're never too old to hear somebody tell you you did a good job. For somebody to show you that they really corrected the mistakes in your work and they didn't just skim through it. I always felt when I was younger, my teacher cared more when I was in elementary school when I made mistakes. Because when I got to middle and high school, I didn't have that many mistakes. But now being in college with my Education Department and they show me all the mistakes I make, it's like, "Wow. I really need help in certain areas."

In my future classroom, the learning looks very active. Active because one thing that I do not like that the school district took out of schools was recess. I feel the kids don't get that time to actually get up, play around, interact with each other, have social skills. So one thing that I will integrate into my curriculum is this guided discovery. So when you use guided discovery in the classroom, it's when the child actually discovers for themselves the answer. You don't just give it to them. You know, like okay, some things will have to be direct instruction. But when you use guided discovery, I think that's more effective.

And then when you use teamwork, I never knew that teamwork wasn't just okay, we all just put in the answer. So in my classroom now, I want to break it down. When I do teamwork, it's not just everybody will get their own role. It's different types of teamwork. I never knew that either. I just think for me having the experience from being in the Education Department at Carver, I really learned how to really control the classroom. I know how to teach things in different ways. I don't just use one way of teaching no more.

So definitely different learning styles, different ways of teaching and I'm just big on the classroom, what the classroom looks like, the way I present it to the children. Presentation is everything for me. In order for my students to do what's best for them, I have to stay on top of myself. So definitely it will be not just them learning but me learning new things too. The more I know, the more I will be able to teach them. That's what I believe.

I see my classroom definitely as a family. The reason why I use the word *family* is because family will always play a key role in everyone's life. I don't care what no one says. Everybody wants to feel like they have a family. If it were up to me, my students' parents would definitely be involved. Between me, the parents and the students, that's how I would build my family. I'm going to always have a parent wall just for my parents. One thing that I learned from my field experience, I might try to put together something once a month for my parents to come in.

If the parents felt like they had a bigger role in school, they probably would do more. Because the way the parents feel today in this generation is like, my child has to go to school. So they've got to do what they've got to do so they can learn. But if I made it seem like it's something for them to learn too, it would just make it better. It would make the family come closer, you know? So I just want a family environment definitely.

After I graduate from Carver, I plan on first getting a job in the Philadelphia school district working in an urban school. I really, really want to work in a Promise Academy.[22] I want to make the difference in a Promise Academy. I don't like the way they're being ran right now. I don't like how—to me a Promise Academy is a CP school[23] right now. I don't like that at all. So I definitely don't want my kids to feel like they're in CP just without the crayons and not bringing book bags.

I want to go to the high-need schools, period. That's not an option. My boyfriend, we argue all the time because he's like, "No. I want you to work at private school. They'll treat you better or work in charter school." It's like urban school is not an option, not for our future kids, not for nothing. And I'm just like, why not? He's like, "Because I'm a police officer, and I get to see firsthand," and he don't want me to work with high schools. He thinks the high school students going to beat me up. But the middle school students is not going to beat me up. It's like he's so scared of urban schools. But it's not an option. I'm going to work in an urban school. And I keep trying to explain to him for me having a background from me studying education, all urban schools are not bad schools. And there we go—key word *urban*. He don't know how to use the word correctly.

I plan on one day having a family too, but it just all depends on where my classroom is at, I want to see my classroom succeed. That's my plan. I plan to be somebody's favorite teacher five years after graduation. If I teach high school, I would see my first graduating class because I want to teach ninth grade. Even if I teach eighth grade, I would see my first graduation class. But in my career, I just want to be set as in do I want to go to charter school or do I really want to stay in urban? Because it's some things that I like about when it comes to staff. I like the way charter schools are ran. But I want to help the children in the urban schools.

I don't equate charter and urban together. I don't know why. I just think charter schools are different. The reason why I don't equate them the same is because in charter schools all the teachers don't have to be certified. So I was just like well, that's different than charter school, when it comes to school choice, they have the choice to turn you away if they don't want you there no more. And then it's lotteries in charter schools. I always put charter school in a different category. I think charter schools—personally, I think they're better. I would put my child in a charter school. I think they're the better public school.

Also, I'm on my way to starting to get a master's. If not by then, if not by five years, definitely when I'm on the sixth year definitely. I want to just further my education. One thing that I learned about education is it's so much more deeper than just getting a bachelor's degree. Without a doubt, I want to be a doctor. I want to have a higher education than my boyfriend. He only have an associate's, and I feel like me being called Dr. Shironda or Dr. Noore not compared to Officer Noore, it just would be better.

I'm going to start my own nonprofit organization within 20 years for young women. Then I want to start a boys program. Because one thing about me and my boyfriend, we're really big on helping. Like too big sometimes. Nonprofit organizations would definitely be the best for us, and he's real big on starting one for young men so like a brothers and sisters connection or something but that's definitely something I know we both see eye-to-eye on. I feel like I missed so many years before that 20 years from now, I'm just beginning.

****

Shironda's passion and dedication to urban education was quite strong. She was one teacher education major caught in the cycle of, "just one more semester, and I can pass the basic skills exam." Although Shironda had top grades and was president of the Honors Society and the Education Club, she still struggled to pass the exam.

Eventually, Shironda switched majors to English. The School District did not revoke her $10,000 scholarship for teacher education, so Shironda, unlike most Carver students, graduated with zero college debt. After graduation, Shironda attended a large university in the Philadelphia area to get her master's degree in English. She has a new boyfriend and is soon to be married.

Dana

When I think of Dana, I immediately think of ginger ale. The day of this interview was Dana's 21st birthday, and we went out to eat at P.F. Chang's to conduct the interview. It was a special day and a major milestone in her life, and Dana insisted on getting just a ginger ale.

This fizzy drink is also a great description of Dana, as it is the soft drink most people turn to when they are sick. Dana was also this person for her friends and colleagues. She was often an open ear and a shoulder of support for many in the education program. Coupled with her radiant smile, Dana was often the source of calmness and reason for many. Dana is an extremely intelligent woman, although she is very humble. A Philadelphia native, she majored in Early Childhood and Elementary Education. In class, Dana was a very attentive student, always listening and processing the information presented. But, she also had a great sense of humor and would bring a positive energy into the classroom.

Dana's journey to teaching was not linear. She came to Carver University as a biology major with aspirations to be a doctor. She did very well in the major, but eventually, Dana started listening to the call to become a teacher.

Home

It's my mom, my younger brother, my great grandmom, and my aunt. My brother's eight years younger than me, so he's 13. My great grandmom, she's retired. My grandmom passed a couple years ago, but my great grandmom's the oldest in the family. I've lived in Philly all my life. We did move during that time, but it was a different neighborhood. It was only around the corner, but different spectrum of the city. So it was a different environment. We went from a quiet setting to a kid directed, noisy, a lot of kids, a lot of noise neighborhood.

So, I pretty much grew up in a family of all women. My brother, he was the only boy since my grandfather. He's actually adopted. That's it though, as far as male influences. I talk to my dad. I kind of think our relationship is stronger now than it was when I was younger, but he just recently moved to Delaware.

When I was born, my mom was 23 and my dad was 34. They met because they worked together. They were both in the post office, and he actually has two other daughters, my two sisters. The middle sister, she is still in the area, but my older sister she is not. The middle sister lives in the Philadelphia area. She works with kids for a Head Start program. She's one of the directors, and she's a single parent of two sons. One is about to graduate high school this year.

My mom, she graduated from high school, and she was the first person in her family to go to college. She went to Millersville University and then being the first person to go to college, my grandmom didn't really know how to prepare for her funding for college, so she had to drop out and she enlisted in the Navy. So she got an undergrad degree from the Navy. Then she had went back to school and got her master's in social work from the University of Pennsylvania. She now works with kids. The jobs I remember her being is she was the director of a community center in North Philadelphia for many years, and now she works with a nonprofit organization that works with public schools and she's still the director of a day-care center. My dad, he still works for the post office.

K–12 Educational Experiences

I went to all private schools. So elementary, I started at this school called Malik Academy. It was an Afrocentric background school. It was a good school, but my mom took me out of there because my mom and my third-grade teacher didn't see eye-to-eye and her teaching style.

At Malik, I wanna say that for each class there was maybe about 20 students. K–8. The actual school was real small. When you look at it from the outside, you might think it was a little medium-size house. So the school was intimate, and it was a real close community school. But as soon as I graduated, my school was closed down.

Then I left there and went to Parisian Academy. It was a Catholic school, so it was a whole entire different atmosphere for me. The discipline was real strict. There was a difference in race when I first got there. When I started, it was mixed. We had everybody from Indian, racial backgrounds. So it was real diverse when I started. By the time I graduated, it was predominantly Black. I'm not sure why because the location of the school is in a middle-class neighborhood. Like big houses and things like that. So I'm not sure why it changed.

I would say all of my schools were teacher-centered. I can't remember a lot of the cooperative learning. I don't remember things like that in elementary school. And eighth grade because, of course, when I first started Parisian, my mom actually had me tested for a learning disability. Come to find out that I was dyslexic. I found out when I was in fourth grade. So Parisian had this learning center for students with disabilities. It was basically a resource room. So, I was there for fourth grade and then that was kind of one-on-one learning, instructional learning, but mostly it was teacher-centered though.

I went to Resource Room for math and reading, and I came back to class for science, social studies, and religion. I tested out of math, and then I still went there for reading and then by my fifth-grade year, I was in school inclusion. I didn't have to go to the Resource Room.

The one teacher that stands out is my fifth-grade special education teacher for reading. Because, even though I was in the learning center for special education, the teachers, they basically had us believe we would also be in the learning center, like there was no way out. She kind of opened our minds that you can go forth and go to the general education room if you wanted to, if we work hard. So, she had a big influence and that we could really leave the learning center and go to general education.

My eighth-grade teacher, Miss Hanna, she had a reputation of being the worst teacher ever. So when I got to seventh grade, I was expecting her head turning around [*laughter*]. So when I first got her, I was like, "Okay, she's mean. Let me see what she's like." Somehow she saw that I had potential, and she was the one who told me to go to this advanced math.

She influenced me to start the advanced math. Miss Hanna worked one-on-one with us. There was only three of us for advanced math. So she worked with us real close and then she would talk to my mom about what high school I should go to and what high school is best for me. She recommended me for the scholarship to high school. That's actually why I went to St. Mary's Catholic School 'cause of the scholarship I received. So I guess, in that way, she influenced me. Both teachers had kind of the same meaning in my life. They told me I could go far. I don't have to stay back in the regular. I could just work hard, and I could do it.

Then I went to an all girls' Catholic high school called St. Mary's. It's a small high school compared to the other high schools in the neighborhood. It's predominantly Hispanic and then Caucasian and then Asian. Actually, African Americans has the lowest percentage in the school. It was like 1% or 2%. It was real low.

Then as I went to eighth grade, I took a section of a general education math class. So the teacher had the advanced math and the average math workers, and then people who need additional help with math. I was there for math because I was a part of the advanced math. It was kind of amazing how I went from the learning center to the advanced math in a short time.

I would say from seventh through high school, that's when I started becoming more A and B. When I went to high school, I was on the honor roll for all my years of high school. I was getting more As and Bs at the high school.

In elementary throughout middle school, I was a part of the newspaper organization. I was a writer for the newspaper. Out of school, I was into sports. I used to play basketball. I used to be on the basketball team, and then I swam.

Carver University

First, my aunt went to Carver, and she graduated with a chemistry degree. Only reason why I went to Carver is because I always knew that Carver had a real, real, real nice-size apartments. When I graduated from high school, I knew I wanted to be a doctor. Well, actually Xavier was my first choice. Then Katrina had happened so yeah, that was off my list. I knew I wanted to go to an HBCU because I went to a predominantly White high school. So, that was very important that I wanted an HBCU.

Then I went to a counselor, and we went all over the northeast region, down south HBCU college tours. Some of my top schools were like Howard, Spelman. I visited the schools, and I realized what I needed for my learning, I needed something intimate and small because I always been in a small school setting. So I knew that the big schools were out of the question. So, then there was Carver and that's when I started to realize that I like Carver because it wasn't too far from home and it had a small environment and the education—the science department was phenomenal. So that's why I picked Carver.

By going to Carver then, by being that it's so small, the teachers can really work one-on-one with you and get that student environment and because most of my teachers, especially for the Education Department, they really became like, I won't say parents, but like mentors in my life for education. Even with sciences, they're on your side.

Then the friends and the social life too, you really have to make your friends, but I expected that 'cause Carver is so small. So far, it's been great. I've got a chance to meet different people from different cities and different backgrounds. It's cool because even though when people look at us, we're so different from our backgrounds and things like that, but on the outside we're similar because we all wanted to reach the children and be important for kids itself. I think that most of my education friends our bond is stronger.

I came to Carver as a bio major. I switched from biology to chemistry because one of my advisors suggested that it would be better for me to go to chemistry than biology. At first, I didn't really see teaching in my career. I wanted to be a doctor, OB/Gyn. I wanted to have something to do with kids 'cause I wanted to become an OB/Gyn, but I wanted to work mainly with teenage girls. So, I guess after I found out that science wasn't really my thing, it was more as a chore than something I had passion for and interest in.

But that's the reason I switched from bio to health science 'cause I knew I wanted to work still with teenagers. I didn't have a glimpse of inspiration or insight that I could do teaching in order to reach out to kids to become the positive model for kids 'cause I always wanted to work with adolescents, that I should start out being a positive influence on when they younger. So, that's where it goes into becoming a teacher.

Looking back, actually I had the African American Experience class with Dr. Edgar, and we were talking about how our children are not being taught the proper Black history with the stories within the textbook, the regular textbook. So that gave me insight that I could be that person or that insight or that teacher to those students so they know who they are, where they came from, where their ancestors came from, and so that will help them become better people. Hopefully, they can work hard so they have that inspiration that they knew where their history and ancestors came from that they could work hard. They could have the encouragement to let them know that they can do it. Nobody can hold them back for anything.

When I told my friends I wanted to be a teacher, at first, they were kind of happy and were like, "It's about time. You didn't know you like to work with kids?" I used to work with kids every summer. I never had a dull job working at the store when I was in high school. I always worked with summer camps and day cares. I always worked with kids throughout my years. So my friends, they just were like, "Okay, it took you this long to discover this?!" My mom, she's a different person. Basically she wanted me to continue with the sciences. Basically, she didn't want me to struggle financially 'cause teachers don't get paid that much for all that they do, but I think she came on the other side when I told her my full plan of teaching. So, I guess my mom, she figured I have a plan. Then I think as she was thinking that when I first thought I was gonna be education, she thought that I was running away from science because it was getting too hard, but when I told her my career goals I guess she realized that I was being serious.

I'll have to say passing [the basic skills exam], though, I'm struggling with the reading section. I guess is that I don't wanna say my dyslexia, but there always has been a struggle for me, and math has always been my stronger point. So I wasn't really too worried about math, but it was reading. I really had to practice with that. And since I'm not a good standardized test taking person, that's the only thing I worried about.

Teaching Career

At first, I wanted to teach for a couple of years, and then I wanna be a principal for another couple years. Then my awesomest goal is to become a superintendent. I wanted to become a superintendent of an urban school district. In our Introduction to Education class, we talk about how a lot of leaders in education in the world are businessmen and -women, and there is not people who have backgrounds in education. So they don't know how to reach out to kids in those type of levels that somebody with education major or background to do. So that's my big ultimate goal.

I'm considering specializing in special education. It's a positive experience because after having two special education courses and looking back on my experience with special education, I kind of wanted to be like the teacher I had to other students. Sometimes I have doubts about can I really run an entire classroom with 30-something kids, but that comes and goes, but everything else is alright.

I wanted to start working with fifth graders 'cause I thought that fifth grade was the most important year. So at first, I wasn't really into the school thing until I got into fifth grade. So, I think fifth grade was the most important grade to see how the students wanna react or feel about the education further, but after doing my sophomore field experience, working with fifth grade, now I wanna work with first graders. Because I worked in a fifth-grade classroom, and then mostly the average kids read on the second-grade level, and they were fifth grade. So that's why I wanted to start in first grade because I think first grade is when they actually start on reading comprehension.

I just wanted to be an advocate, most important a mentor to the students 'cause I can see from experience because fifth grade I was not really into school at all. I didn't like to read. It was school was there because my mom and everybody said that you have to go to school. So once I left fifth grade, that's when my whole mindset changed. So I think that's the most important age to determining the success of the students in elementary school.

One of my goals is for all my students to be, not advanced, but a little ahead of their grade level in every subject. So when they continue to other grades, they don't have to struggle and feel like they haven't been taught.

I think teaching looks like not just a teacher dictating to the students, but everybody's being involved, everybody's having fun 'cause my expression of teaching is, "if there's nothing that you can relate to or to break it down easily, you're not gonna get it." I want my classroom learning environment to be constant. Like you learn from anything, from having a regular conversation with your classmate or learning is just constant, always, and you can learn anything. Anything new every minute.

In terms of my future influences on learning, I see me being more creative, stepping out of the box and don't be afraid to look like a fool, even though you might feel like, "Okay, I might look real dumb, but as long as the students, they enjoy it," but what's important is that they get the information.

I know I want my students to come to me in any type of situation, if they have questions in any situation at all, family, school related and know that they can come to me even if they're not in my classroom. I want for them to be comfortable with themselves so they're comfortable with people around them. I don't wanna be like I'm the teacher, you're the student. But then I don't want them to be, "Oh, that's my best friend," but I also want them to know that I'm always there for them in any situation possible. Just know you can come to me if anything. I guess an open relationship.

I feel that a relationship with the parents are the most important thing kids need to have. I want the parents to lean on me any time of the day, but just for any questions about their student. I just want basically the same type of relationship with the students, but on a higher level.

I really want basically the same type of relationship that I have with my classmates in the Education Department with my colleagues. If they have any creative or a fun lesson plan to talk to me, and we can work and share and collaborate. Collaborate with one another because if the whole school is altogether for the kids, than the kids will feel that. They will wanna do better. They have a sense of a warm atmosphere. So I guess working together is a key ingredient to be a effective teacher.

I wanna work at a private school in the urban environment just because I don't think they have enough effective teachers. Then I see myself, while still teaching, getting my principal's certification and hopefully becoming the principal of that school. I wanna still stay in the urban school district. I guess my whole life career is evolving around urban education. After I receive my superintendent certification, I would hope to move to Atlanta, but for right now I still wanna stay in Philadelphia because Philly still needs effective teachers, real good teachers.

Five years after graduation, I've taken classes to get my principal's certification. I see my classroom and then not just the classroom, but like a community, like a second home to students. I see myself having maybe a mentoring club or organization for girls. Not just for teaching, but I see myself doing different programs. Maybe one child and a house and a nice neighborhood in Philadelphia.

I think 10 years out my life and career will be basically the same as five years, but I guess on a different higher level. I wanna work with getting my superintendent's certification. Then hopefully my girls' mentoring program will go citywide; not just from our school, but from different schools and different districts for young girls.

Twenty years out, hopefully I am either a superintendent for Philadelphia public schools or Atlanta. Real focused on making education the lead for every student, every grade. Probably working with, still females, young girls, but maybe older, a little bit more older. Maybe college age so that, especially young women and men who is interested in education, because then I will have the experience underneath my belt so I could teach more wisely and, maybe be a professor on the side.

****

Dana was a focused and determined student. With much work, she did successfully pass the reading basic skills portion of the teacher certification. She, unlike most of the stories in this book, graduated from Carver University as a certified teacher.

As promised, Dana moved back to Philadelphia to be a teacher. She currently teaches fifth graders at a Catholic school in the city, and she has been teaching for three years. On a personal note, Dana has also grown her family, and she is a new mom to a baby girl.

· 6 ·

SENIOR YEAR: CERTIFIED TEACHER

Claresha

One day in my office, I was briefly having a conversation with Claresha while another one of my students, Keshawn, was waiting to talk with me. After Claresha left, Keshawn closely watched Claresha leave the office and then said, "Who was THAT, Doc?" This was often the response many men had to Claresha, as she is a dynamic natural beauty. Tall and lanky, she would wear her hair in twists, and she really could pass for Erykah Badu's baby sister. Often, she would come to class in a colorful, funky, retro outfit that was capped off with bright green Converse sneakers.

Claresha's creative side would come out in many ways. My colleague, one day, saw her riding a long-board skateboard around campus. He exclaimed, "What Black girl does that?" but it was not surprising to any of us that it was Claresha, as she would often dance to the beat of her own drum. As an avid poet, Claresha would use amazing imagery when she talked or completed papers in class. Her spirit for teaching and her love for English were prevalent within the university classroom. A well-read individual, Claresha would often talk about finding different methods to connect reading to the ninth graders in her urban field experience class.

Claresha was a Secondary Education, English major at Carver University. Originally from a White, middle-class neighborhood in Maryland, Claresha had intentions of being an Afrocentric-based teacher—something she lacked in her schooling experiences.

Home

I was born outside of DC in a newly developing suburb. But then it was very rural. There wasn't even McDonald's. We were the only Black family on the block. So it's me, my two sisters. I'm in the middle. My older sister is about four years older than me; my youngest is about two years younger. My mother, my father, and my maternal grandmother. That was basically my family from birth till about middle school.

Although we were the only Black family, they decided to move there because they came from pretty rough backgrounds in the city, inner city DC, I guess you would call it—that basically that idea of trying to break the cycle of poverty that a lot of Black people or people of color first- or second-generation immigrants to the country, wanna break that cycle of poverty that has been goin' on in past generations. So they thought move into a new place, start anew, with a good school system and all that would be beneficial for the children.

We went to church on the weekends in the city and that was our dose of Black culture, but for the most part I was kind of isolated from it in my childhood until middle school. I say this because it's kind of like important concerning my educational experience, my different cultural interactions with different groups.

My grandmother was a large role 'cause she went to school to be a teacher. She went to an HBCU, but she couldn't afford to finish, but she drilled us on our ABCs and our 1, 2, 3s. She was always there. We never had to go into day care or anything like that 'cause she was always there. So she always helped us with our homework. Sometimes she did our homework because she was such a perfectionist and that kind of rubbed off on us as well. So we always had a tutor, and my mom, she worked a job. She was able to work part-time, and she worked close by. We had our problems, but had a good foundation. I was always around my family. My older sister taught me how to write. That's why I'm a lefty. So I had a good educational start.

When I was 11, fifth grade, my parents divorced. They'd been fighting and all that, but they finally split, and we moved into a nice little apartment meaning me, my sisters, my grandmother, and my mom. We all lived in a two-bedroom apartment. Then it was just like, "Eh." So that was my family. Just the women.

Up until about 10th grade or 11th grade, my mom kinda dated in between. My stepfather came into the picture about my junior year. During this time, it was a really pivotal point of my adolescence. It was just women. Then my mom remarried kind of late in my teens and also my dad remarried. The family that was just two girls now I have a stepsister, two stepbrothers, and then four younger brothers and sisters from my dad's side.

When the divorce happened, we only moved around the corner so I saw my dad on weekends, but then things kind of went sour. My dad kinda had a crisis of his manhood so he kinda ran away and moved to the Midwest—Indiana. He went there, and he went to North Carolina. So he was not a part of my life during those years. We're kind of rebuilding now, but he wasn't there. When they divorced, he was pretty much out of the picture. He moved back to Maryland recently.

My parents met in church. They were really religious. They got married really young. They got married when my mom was 19. My dad was like 20. So they were really into the church, the church I grew up in when we lived in DC. When they met, he was a preacher for a while. He was a preacher of a church and that's really what brought them together, their religion. They were Christian.

My mother, she took a few classes at the community college, but she was an accountant for many years and that's her specialty. She does clerical work. And my dad, he took up a trade. He was an electrician for 20 years. Now he's moving into project management, site management.

My oldest sister went to an HBCU, she was the first to graduate with a bachelor's in our immediate family. She went for business and fashion merchandising. At first, she worked for the people that own Macy's and Bloomingdale's. She did a corporate thing, but she hated it. So now she's transitioned into freelance. She works at a bar or club on the weekends and does parties. My youngest sister also goes to Carver for business and entrepreneurship. She did cosmetology in high school, like vocation. I think she wants to open up a salon or somethin' of that sort.

K–12 Educational Experiences

Downy Elementary, named after Captain Downy who was a fallen soldier. He was a cop who was killed. I forget where he was killed. He was on duty, and he was killed. That's who my school was named after. We went to his memorial and learned about Captain Downy, and it was so much fun!

It was a very good school. It had a lot of rigorous courses, and we even had Spanish classes, we could take Spanish classes in the morning. We came early to take Spanish. I remember doing that. I remember we always had computers and those big ol' floppy discs, and we played the Oregon Trail.

It was a big school. There was a Head Start there, too. So it was Head Start through sixth at first—well, when my older sister was there. Then it changed from Head Start through fifth. Sixth was junior high and middle school.

When I was at Downy, I was recommended for special services. First of all, let me say I hated school, and I did not wanna go 'cause my older sister went to a Hebrew school and she woke up at like the butt crack of dawn to go. She was three years old when she started 'cause she had a Head Start. It was a private school, and I did not wanna go. I hated wakin' up in the morning, but when I got to kindergarten, I went to p.m. kindergarten. I loved Ms. O'Reilly. She was so sweet. I loved her.

First grade though, the teacher wasn't as warm. I just wasn't learning in her class, and they recommended me for services. A reading specialist would come pull me out and they told my mom. She's like, "Yeah, give her all the help she can get." The teacher was an African American lady. I remember that room like it was yesterday and fun. It had like stuff everywhere and always got treats and goodies. I was like, "Ah, I like this." Then I improved. My pullout services ended in fourth grade. When I started doing well, they took me out. So I feel she was an influence on me, too. Then I had really good teachers at Downy. It was a really good start for me, really good teachers. The administration was good, too. It was a really good, warm atmosphere.

I remember in elementary school, it was fun. I remember this one class, Miss Jenkins, second grade, I wanna do this so bad with my class, but I have to figure out how. She built community in a stone town or something like that, and we all had jobs. I still have my little card. We had little cards. I was the fireman. I put the fireman hat on, took my picture, and I was the fireman in the town. There was a police officer. We all had a role.

I felt like when I walked in that classroom, I was in another world. Like you as a child, your imagination's so broad. I felt like it was a safe place for learning and then, she didn't take any stuff either. She gave me that look one day and I was like, I still remember that look till this day. She was sweet as pie, but you don't mess with her, right. That's why I liked it. So it was different. I felt I was a part of that learning environment. So it got more and more teacher-centered. Fifth grade was much more like direct teaching. I guess getting us ready for middle school.

When I was there, I had friends of color, different cultures, but mostly White. I don't remember being different. I never remember feeling badly about myself or feeling that the kids were mean to me because I was Black. They were really open actually. My mom later told me that parents were sometimes kind of, "Eh," but as a kid you don't really see that or you shouldn't see that.

I never got that sense, except when I got to fifth grade, and I was the only Black girl in the class. I kinda started to feel it, and I guess being older and almost in that adolescent age and when they talk about Black people, people would look at me. I started to feel socially that isolation, but the kids were actually really nice. They're like, "Ya' know, I feel bad that that happened in class today. I feel bad that you really got focused on in class." I remember them being really nice to me actually.

Middle school was Naron and that was a whole other story. Middle school was really different. This was when my parents divorced, and I remember sleeping on the floor one night when my dad first left. It was a really traumatic, emotional time for me. Then going to school and there was more diversity at Naron. I'll say that, and that's a good thing. The school got matriculated inward. Germantown where I grew up, the White part of town and right next to it is Montgomeryville is where I live now and Gaithersburg. There's more people of color, more people that lived there and more diversity. I hung out with just the students of color, and I began to see that discrepancy and separation, and we were all different. We had to all kinds of people of color. Some were Hispanic or Black and some White people hung out with us, but still majority White.

I remember our group was being targeted all the time by administration, I guess if we were loud and rowdy, but we're 11 and 12 years old. Whenever we're in the lunchroom, "Hey, be quiet." We're just like, "Uh, leave us alone, please. We just like to have fun." I guess maybe we were really bad and we deserved it. I don't know, but at the time we felt really persecuted. We didn't deserve it. We were different.

That was the first time I had, in sixth grade, a teacher say something blatantly racist. It was my art teacher and mind you, I really liked this teacher. She was a young White girl. She had to be fresh out of college. She was really nice, and she's was kind of like artsy and hippie and out there, which made me all the more surprised that she would say something like she did. She told this one kid, Alex, who was an African American, I guess he was bein' lazy or she thought he wasn't givin' his all on this one art project, and she said, "Oh, you don't wanna be like another one of these Black kids on the streets, do you?" Or she said something to that nature, like you don't wanna end up like those other Black guys.

The whole class stopped and just looked at her. I was like—steam was probably just coming from my ears, but I was so mad and I didn't know what to say or who to say it to. So I just internalized it 'cause I never had experienced that before. She's like, "What?! What?!," like she didn't understand what she had said, but it was pretty bad.

In fifth grade, I was the only Black in the class. That was the case because I was tracked in the highest class. I know some of my other friends were probably in the lower class, and they were hangin' out the door and havin' fun. We were reading novels, small novels and learning about past participles and it's just going right over my head. So I was tracked into a lower-achieving English class in sixth grade as a result. 'Cause I got like two Ds in fifth grade.

Then for my behavior, I stayed in a lower-achieving English class in seventh grade. That's when Miss Gray—I remember her to this day. I love her. She's like a Irish lady. She reminded me of Miss O'Reilly. She was like an older White lady, and she had like short, curly hair with the White hair that's curled.

I remember this day like it was yesterday. She asked, "What's different about this sentence?" I looked at it and everybody's like, "Nah, nah, nah." I'm like, "It's a compound sentence." She said, "Why?" And I explained to her why because they can be two separate sentences if they want to be. She's like, "You need to see me." Pulled me aside after class and said, "You don't need to be in this class. You're very intelligent. I'm recommending you for the highest class, one of my classes and I'm gonna recommend you for a GT, which is gifted and talented next year." That is a moment that totally changed my educational career 'cause I have always written poetry. I've always been a writer, and that kind of affirmed in me my strength in English and that, "Okay, this is my thing."

So eighth grade, I was in gifted and talented. My behavior was still a problem because I was going through so much at home, but I was a good student. I got in a fight in seventh grade and got ISS, in school suspension. I would verbally flip out on teachers sometimes if they deserved it. The principal and vice principal, Mr. Anderson. He was Irish and had all these freckles, I mean, all these freckles. I used to hate them. But then Miss

Nando was like our hero. She was the sweetest thing, and she took me aside and she said, "Ya' know, you gotta do what you have to do. Ya' know what my dad did to me when I was acting up?" She said, "He put me in all honors classes." She said, "You can fail out if you wanted, but …" She was just tellin' me all these things and encouraged me. So she was also a good mentor.

I don't remember any cooperative learning in middle school really. Maybe that's why we were so bored and rowdy. Teacher-directed. High school, same thing. Not a lot of diversified instruction or anything like that. Probably neglected it as we got older. I don't know why.

My high school was Gaterville High School. We had a graduating class of 400. We moved to the next town over. So I went to a new high school. So I didn't go to high school with my elementary and middle school buddies. It was a totally new high school. I only knew one girl there. The school was really diverse. All types of people. I'd say mostly White, Blacks, and Hispanics, but I had friends who were Arabic, Indian, from Africa, born in Africa, everybody. So it was really diverse, and I liked that.

When I came in, I didn't know anybody. I'm not really the type to make friends, walk up to people I don't know. So my freshman year I was just silent. I took honors classes. I took honors history, honors English of course, whatever subjects I felt strongly in. I took honors. I kept my head down and did my work and got really good grades and that was my freshman year. I didn't even go to a football game or anything. I just didn't know anybody, and I wasn't really active.

But my sophomore year, I tried out for cheerleading and that helped me kind of get into the scene. I figured out I'm not really that social, but if I involve myself in a lot of things, I'll meet people 'cause that's a way for me to build confidence and do that. I just kept on taking honors classes, more honors. Honors science; I'll try that now, even though it's not really one of my favorite subjects. I took AP Composition; AP English in 11th grade; AP Literature in 12th, and I took AP Psychology.

I got As and Bs. Different times, like 11th grade I did really well. I did like all 4.0 and 3.85; I did 3.85s and one B. I don't know how many classes I was taking. Senior year, I kinda slacked off. I did not do well at all. 'Cause I already knew what I wanted to do afterwards so I was kinda over it. I've always gotten good grades. All As and Bs mostly. Cs seldom.

I started extra activities mostly in high school, cheerleading. I did gymnastics. I did track. I did student government. I did a debutante program.

Carver University

My high school teacher went to Carver, so it's kind of nice to have that Carver connection. She'll talk to me about Carver, and when she found out I was applying and going. Actually through her college fair is how I applied for Carver and talked to the admissions representative, and she pulled some strings to get me a scholarship so that was really important.

I was drafted for the honors program here at Carver. They got us right transition week.[24] It was like, "You have good grades. You're in the honors program." So I've been in that all four years.

The teacher education program has been frustrating, rewarding, educational, and mostly rewarding and frustrating. Frustrating because of all the requirements and stressing about getting out and doing what you have to do. I remember getting that letter in the mail that says, "You are not an education major because you don't have A, B, C, or D." It was like a laundry list of crap. Like you haven't taken a math, the basic skills exam, it was just like, "Eh." I went into Dr. Watson's office and was like, "I don't wanna be an education major. I'll just graduate and go to Graduate School." He was like, "No, don't do that." He calmed me down and said, "You'll be fine."

I think we need to be in the field more and mocking lessons more and simulating, really getting up and delivering lessons because that's what you're gonna be doing, and you don't wanna get to student teaching and just having observed and sat back and then all of a sudden you're thrown to the wolves and you're like, "I don't know." You're not gonna be sure, but I think it will help.

What's rewarding is just working toward becoming an educator. Because that's what I wanna do. And meeting professors that are really inspiring me to be an educator and tell me I can do it even when I'm kind of, "Eh," kind of out of it.

And I love being with the kids. Like I observed at Ogontz[25] before I did Perkins.[26] Perkins was really rewarding and working with the kids was great and observing in Ogontz was just like a totally different atmosphere because it's rural. It's mostly White, but the kids are still so accepting of me. They just like to have a new voice in the class, a new face.

I try to be friends with other educators that are already working and get their opinions and advice. It's always good to be friends with other educators. There are certain things that other people just—it's natural. They're not gonna understand it if they're not in that culture I guess. I love it. All the education majors really have a passion for it, you always have that connection with them and you'll be able to talk about things. There's a lot to it. A lot of things that you need to tell the younger majors ones about. Like, "Hey, take [the basic skills exam] now," and if they do this, then yeah.

Teaching Career

I was thinking about the time where my mom was like, "What do you wanna do? What are you gonna do?" I was in my sophomore year of high school. "What are you gonna do after high school?" And I'm really thinking about, "Well, what do I wanna do with my life?" My mom did all these different programs, like you answer all these questions and they match you to a different career. I list all my strengths and weakness and my likes and dislikes and try to figure out what career I wanna choose.

I just hated school. I always did well, but I hated school because of my experiences with crappy teachers. I had good teachers, but the crappy ones—the bad stuff kind of always outweighs the good in a child's mind. But somehow teaching just fit. My strength was English. That was my subject. I was a really good writer. I love to write. And I wanted to help people. I really wanted to change my life to something that would benefit others. I wanted to help other people, and I put the two together and got English teacher.

So, I fought it for a while. Like, "No, I don't wanna do that," but it's kind of like a calling, like grasping my faith. All this stuff you didn't like about your teachers or school, you can be different and bring something different to your school. So it kind of evolved that way.

With my stepdad, he worries about me teaching in the city. My parents worry about me making enough money. They're like, "You kind of need that and you need to make more money." They're really worried about me living in the city. My mom, she's been out of the city so long, like we moved in '88. She's been moved out from the city and urban life and lived in the Black community for so long that she's has of fear and her experiences when she was younger, like she might have a reason to fear if she thinks it's like the way it was when she was younger, her neighborhood. So they're kind of iffy in my interest in urban education. All my friends are education majors, so they're supportive [*laughter*]. But the ones that aren't, they see it for me and are like, "I could never do it, but you'll do it well."

My primary goals as a teacher change every day. As a teacher, I wanna be able to survive and eat, but I don't really know. I feel like I'm just kind of goin' for it just like how I went for being a teacher. Just kind of going for teaching my goals, my ultimate goal is to be effective and to be able to integrate culturally, raise cultural awareness in my classroom and be able to relate to my students, have them relate to literature or whatever it is they're reading or writing and to make it interesting for them and help them, help me. Teaching at Perkins is kind of like a lot of kids, people give up on them 'cause they don't do anything, they're failing, whatever, and a lot of people got so much going on in their lives that they don't have time to really. You can't save everyone, but try to invest that time in them. It will be optimistic, but it's better to shoot for something high than not.

As a teacher,[27] I hope to be effective and be able to relate the curriculum to the realities of my students. I wish to be happy and at least financially stable. Since I've been student teaching, I have further affirmed these goals. I wrestle with curriculum set by the district daily and attempt to squeeze some life and culture into my lessons. But I sense that students are uninterested because public school education does a poor job of addressing the needs of diverse learners and individuals with future goals other than college. When first entering the teacher education program, I had no idea of what to expect. I knew English was my strength and interest and education would be my career. However, I had no idea how to get there! I kind of just jumped in head first without much thought other than doing well in classes and graduating on time. What it was to actually become and develop my "teacher persona" so to speak, was not even a thought.

My future classroom will be a community setting. Similar to that of my second-grade teacher Miss Jenkins, but a secondary version of it. I want my classroom (and hopefully the school I work in) to be a safe haven for learners. Where students can take in knowledge and think critically in a nonthreatening environment. I also want to teach morals and values of respect, support, and encouragement along with life skills that are important for young adults. Many children, even those from "good homes," do not learn many of these skills of professional protocol (writing checks, emailing/mailing a memo or professional letter, résumés, etc.) because of the emphasis on work and career in our society. Many parents are unavailable. This image is affected by such factors as the home and surrounding community, which may discourage supportive learning (or any kind of learning for that matter). The image has not changed much, for I am still idealistic. I have realized that it will be more difficult than expected and will not happen overnight. Especially considering the school I work in most likely will not share this same approach to the classroom. Like I said, at first I had no clue, so since entering the teacher education program and immersing myself in many cultural classes from Black and multicultural psychology, to African American literature, and cultural anthropology, teamed with two summers abroad, I have adapted my view of life and thus education to fit this model. I feel it is more relevant to students of color.

With my future students, I hope to be a figure that beckons respect and warrants love. With my students, I hope to build a relationship that is filled with high expectations and an eagerness to learn from each other. With my colleagues, I hope to have a strong professional relationship. Since I have been student teaching, I also hope to keep my distance in a sense. One must never get too personal with anyone at work or school. There can be a lot of turmoil and mix-up when you subject yourself to gossip and trash-talking students, administrators, faculty, and parents. With parents, I hope to build a very strong connection. Parents are vital in a student's success because academic and behavioral interventions often must be extended into the student's home life in order for any changes to occur. Since being involved in the education program, I have experienced a sort of pessimism that runs rampant throughout the educational field today. The dreaded parents, careless, or overly concerned, shouting, cussing, and insane, or indifferent. Whatever the malice, the student must come first. A priority that has disintegrated (or maybe never existed).

In five years, I see myself possibly starting a family and/or living and teaching abroad for a few years. Maybe doing the Peace Corps. I see myself having my master's as well.

In 10 years, I hope to have my PhD in Black or African Studies. I also hope to have started and sustained an after-school community program, tutoring program, rec center, summer camp (something of the sort) that will eventually develop into a school. I hope to have traveled more by this time and learned Kiswahili and/or isiZulu.

In 20 years, I hope to develop my ideal school: a multicultural epicenter for true education. Students will be immersed in cultural affairs, history, and lifestyles. Students will learn about the world from a culturally sensitive perspective. My school will be an extension of my ideal classroom. A community of learners who seek knowledge and think critically about the world around them in peace and safety. I also hope to get these students traveling abroad on some sort of exchange program to see the world they are learning about.

****

I received an email from a colleague from graduate school about how, after years of planning, she was opening an Afrocentric charter school, and she was looking for English teachers. Immediately, I thought of Claresha and her passion for Afrocentric curriculum. Claresha interviewed and got the job as a ninth-grade English teacher at the school. There was an opening ceremony for the school, and I got to see Claresha at the event. It was at this time that she shaved off the twists in her hair, a sign that this was a new chapter in her life.

Four years later, I saw Claresha at another event at the school. During this time, she was praising and providing critique to the senior students (whom she had as freshman) about their projects. Strong, dynamic, and speaking with such loving authority to her students, I remember thinking, "She has really come into her own as a teacher." This strong voice is also coupled with the poetry readings Claresha performs. Recently, she published her first book of poetry, again showing her creative and brilliant mind. A side, no doubt, she often brings into the classroom.

· 7 ·

WE GOT NEXT: PASSING THE TORCH

These educational life histories shed light on the systematic issues that many Black prospective teachers face when trying to become a teacher. Of the 10 stories here, only three (Tyrone, Dana, and Claresha) preservice teachers became certified teachers and achieved their dreams. Jessica was finally successful by moving states and attending a university that did not have the basic skills certification exam. This was also a costly and time-consuming choice Jessica had to make to become a teacher.

On a larger scale, of the 20 Black preservice teachers interviewed for this project, only one other education major (besides Tyrone, Dana, and Claresha) became a teacher. This preservice teacher, Janessa, actually had to transfer into Carver University from another HBCU so that she had a passing score on the basic skills test. At Carver, her scores met the state's passing requirement, but in her former state, the scores did not. For most of the people highlighted in these pages, dreams were shattered and the light within the torch was smoldered. While reading the narratives for this project, some participants told me that they cried at their dreams not being accomplished.

The roadblocks with the Black prospective teachers unable to pass the basic skills exam or, for some, maintain the 3.0 GPA give light to a bigger national issue—the quality of K–12 education for students in urban areas.

Most of the preservice teachers went to school in urban, public school systems on the East Coast, and it was the gaps in the learning systems there that ultimately affected their abilities to pass this exam. The ones who were able to carry the torch for Black teachers were Tyrone, educated at a boarding school during his early years; Dana, a private school attendee all her life; and Claresha, a middle-class suburban public school student. These three were outliers in terms of their schooling, and these three were the only ones to graduate as certified teachers.

Although Allen willingly switched out of the major and Tanya was a victim of her circumstance with her car accident, Leon, Shironda, and Tierra (and even Jessica) fell prey to the common trap of Black teachers not passing the basic skills exam. Dashawn, on the other hand, was also victimized, but through being misadvised at the university. All four of them wanted to exclaim, "We got next!" and pass the torch, but instead, all of them were benched from being a teacher. Their stories, along with the others not recorded in this book, outlined two themes as to why Black prospective teachers are getting roadblocked from entering the profession: failing K–12 urban, public school systems and the psychological strain of standardized testing.

The failed K–12 urban, public school system is demonstrated clearly in Shironda's story. As a child, she loved school, but that quickly changed with the unsafe and unsupportive middle school she attended. Shironda fell rapidly and unnoticed through the cracks. Through high school and college, Shironda had been trying to play "catch up" with her reading and writing abilities. As she admitted in her story, she can easily hide her weaknesses, but the wounds of the failed school system are still there. Her story is one of many I came across during this project. There was Khalil, a straight-A student who learned to accommodate for his undiagnosed dyslexia by himself. His kindergarten teacher noticed it early on, but he was never classified, and teachers would just pass him off to the next grade. He, too, was unable to pass the basic skills exam and graduate as a certified teacher. This again demonstrates that, like Shironda, Khalil fell through the cracks within the system, and the system's failure had lasting effects on his career choice.

The second theme is the psychological strain of standardized testing. There is no denying that our society greatly values standardized testing to categorize learning. In this case, the basic skills exam, to many, established if people are fit to be a teacher, or not. In these stories, we see the immediate, lasting, and anxiety-ridden effect the test had on these Black prospective teachers. For example, Leon admits that even before taking the test he knew it would most likely prevent him from being a teacher. He wanted to run out of the room during the registration for the test. He "missed" the bus to take the test. There is no mistaking that the exam took a psychological toll on him. We also see this in Claresha's story, where she walked into a faculty member's office wanting to give up because the requirements to be a teacher were too overwhelming for her.

These two themes should make us take pause. There is much literature discussing the "achievement gap" with learning in urban schools, but the cycle is larger and extends itself, as it also affects our pool of teacher candidates. The collection of Black teachers will continue to shrink if the system maintains itself as it does. This year, Carver University has only one preservice teacher who passed the basic skills exam. *One.* Other HBCUs in the South have been closing their doors on their teacher education programs.

It is evident that there is a cry for help for Black teachers to enter into the profession. Something needs to change, and change starts with listening to the voices that want to be a part of the profession.

·AFTERWORD·

AN INVITATION TO DIALOGUE ABOUT THE TEACHING PROFESSION

First and foremost, Lynnette Mawhinney's work chronicling the life histories of African American prospective educators at Carver University carries forward an important tradition of research, initiated more than 15 years ago with Michele Foster's seminal book *Black Teachers on Teaching*, by representing the lives of Black educators with their own words. Contextualized as it is within a Historically Black University, Mawhinney's work sheds light on the experiences, struggles, and successes of prospective Black educators at an institution that prepares the largest number of Black educators in one U.S. state. In this way it brings to the forefront the challenges facing not only this particular group of Black preservice teachers but also the teaching profession as a whole. Just as the life history methodology situates lives within larger historical and social contexts and recognizes teachers' identities as socially constructed, so these teachers' experiences reflect larger trends in the teaching profession today.

The preservice teachers interviewed by Mawhinney have experiences highly reflective of what Susan Moore Johnson (2007) and colleagues have termed the "Next Generation of Teachers." Many of these millennials were educated in re-segregated K–12 schools, with a majority-minority student body. They grew up under the testing and accountability requirements of No Child Left Behind (NCLB) and came of age during the recent economic downturn. Upon expressing a desire to become a teacher, they found a variety of preparation pathways available to them, coupled with at-times opaque and convoluted certification requirements not always clearly understood by the candidates themselves. Many of these educators never made it to the classroom. While nationally close to half of teacher preparation candidates fail to pursue classroom teaching, what is striking about the experiences of these educators is how many fail to complete certification requirements. We learn from their words that their chosen careers often emerge not from a lack of desire to teach but rather from the financial, emotional, and academic costs of teaching's professional demands.

The experiences of the educators captured in Mawhinney's book raise several important questions about the teaching profession. Drawing from the lives of African American teachers included in this book, one of the most salient questions is *Who will be today's teachers?* Despite a decade of policy efforts, a strong achievement gap remains in U.S. schools and Black students in particular fail to reach the same level of achievement as their White counterparts. While teachers of a variety of backgrounds can certainly be successful at educating Black children, the voices expressed in this book raise the question of why is it so difficult for prospective Black educators to complete certification requirements to teach students whose racial and cultural backgrounds reflect their own. Mawhinney notes that only 6% of teachers are African American, far fewer than the correlating percentage of African American students. Certainly this dynamic raises the question of who should be recruited into the teaching profession in years to come.

Second, Mawhinney's work raises the questions *What knowledge and skills should today's teachers hold?* and *How do we assess their effectiveness?* Here again, the voices expressed in Mawhinney's book share a degree of frustration over statewide exams that serve as gatekeepers, preventing prospective educators from pursuing their certification programs. Setting a high academic bar for teachers on one hand raises the level of professionalism in the field. On the other hand, these prospective teachers rightly question the rationale behind a single test limiting their ability to pursue their chosen careers. National and international standards for the preparation of teachers highlight disciplinary content knowledge as only one of many important competencies. The basic skills test discussed by so many of these educators represents a general academic test used as a prerequisite to this disciplinary content knowledge. These educators' experiences certainly raise the question of whether a more inclusive teacher preparation system might incorporate multiple assessments of the broad set of knowledge and skills needed in today's classrooms.

Third, while much of the dialogue surrounding the teaching profession rightly focuses on developing a highly skilled teaching force for our students, the personal and professional needs of the teachers themselves should also be incorporated into the conversation. The voices of these prospective educators do just that when they raise the question *What makes teaching an attractive profession for the current generation?* While many of these educators talk about future relationships with students and mentoring others in the way they themselves were mentored, their words are juxtaposed against the high financial, emotional, and academic costs of pursuing teaching. The academic preparation is costly, the emotional demands are costly, and the academic strains of a failed detour into teaching are costly, particularly given the low pay and prestige afforded to teachers once they formally enter the field. Many of these educators never get the chance to build those mentoring relationships they so desire. As a profession, we should be concerned about how to make teaching an attractive profession that works harder to recruit, prepare, mentor, and sustain educators than keep them out.

Finally, these young educators invite a conversation about *What type of teaching pipeline do we want to construct?* What are the affordances and constraints of the current leaky pipeline, in which many future educators dabble in education coursework but never make it to the classroom or do so for only a brief period of time? How does our current system in the United States compare with the system in countries such as Finland, where teaching is held in high regard and future educators, once they have secured admission into teacher preparation, rarely choose to leave and instead stay on to learn and grow as professionals? Finland has worked out a way to maintain high standards while simultaneously making education an attractive profession. The medical profession in the United States has similarly worked out a way to demand exceptional academic achievement while also enticing many young professionals to join their ranks. Few physicians leave medicine during or after their training. The challenges faced by the African American preservice teachers in Mawhinney's book should provoke a meaningful dialogue about how best to construct professional pipelines and pathways that value teachers while holding them to the highest possible standards for our children.

I thank Lynnette Mawhinney for sharing the voices of these preservice educators and inviting these important conversations about the future of our profession.

Carol R. Rinke
New York

·APPENDIX·
INTERVIEW PROTOCOL

Interview #1: Life History

- What is your name, address, year of birth, marital status (year of marriage), birthplace?*
- Who would you identify as being in your immediate family? How many brothers and/or sisters do you have? Birth order and spacing?*
- How many years did you live in the house where you were born? Has your family moved since then? For what reason did you family make these moves?*
- How old were your parents when you were born? What were their occupations? Work hours? Did they have other jobs before or after they became that? Did they also do any part-time jobs? Do you remember your parents ever being out of work? What are their highest levels of schooling/education? *
- Who looked after the children while your parents were at work?*
- What type of schools did you attend growing up? (public/private/religious/size/student demographics)
- What do you remember about how you were taught in school? (discussion, teacher-directed, student-directed) How did you respond to those methods?

- How did your teachers describe your abilities on your report cards?
- How did you spend your time outside of school? Did you participate in any clubs or sports? Describe your participation (time commitment, intensity, affiliation).
- Were there any teachers, coaches, or other adults who particularly stand out in your mind as influential in your childhood? Describe your relationship with them.
- Did you have any contact with teachers outside of the classroom? What was your interaction with them? What did you think of teachers?
- When did you decide that you wanted to pursue teaching? How did you come to that decision? What were the primarily individuals or events influencing your decision?
- How have your family members, friends, and other important individuals in your life reacted to your decision to teach?

Interview #2: Teacher Education

- Tell me about your decision to attend [Carver University]? How did you make that decision? What were the primary factors influencing your choice? Has the college been what you expected? In what ways does it meet or not meet expectations?
- Tell me about your decision to pursue teacher education. Describe your experiences in the teacher education program at [Carver University]. What have been some of the most defining experiences (either positive, negative, or both)?
- In what ways has teacher education been what you expected? In what ways has it been different?
- Describe your relationship with other students in the teacher education program. Describe your relationship with the faculty, cooperating teachers, and supervisors. Which individuals particularly stand out to you and why?
- What do you consider to be your primary goals as a teacher? What factors have influenced these goals? Have these goals changed since entering the teacher education program? If so, how?
- Describe what the teaching and learning will look like in your future classroom. What factors have influenced this image? Has this image changed since entering the teacher education program? If so, how?

- Describe your relationships with your future students, colleagues, parents, and administrators. What factors have influenced this image? Has this image changed since entering the teacher education program? If so, how?
- How do you envision your career as an educator? Describe where you would like to see yourself 5, 10, and 20 years after graduation. This includes work context (type of school), responsibilities (teaching, coaching, administration, etc.), professional growth, and family situation (marriage, children).

Asterisks indicate the questions were taken from A.S. Johnson's (2007) article.

(Note: This complete interview protocol was published in: Mawhinney, L., Rinke, C., & Park, G. (2012). Being and becoming a teacher: A Road to student advocacy between African-American and White preservice teachers. *The New Educator.* 8(4), 321–344).

NOTES

1. Please note that *African American* and *Black* are used interchangeably.
2. All names and places are pseudonyms to ensure anonymity.
3. Note that this figure was often reported high, as the requirements for academic probation were often lowered. Thus, most Carver students who failed almost all their classes were often "retained" for the following year.
4. The teaching certification guidelines were outlined by the state. But often when students called the state to get permission to student teach because they did not pass the basic skills exam by one point, the state would deny that they were the ones to outline the certification guidelines and blame that teacher education program, which was just following the state's laws.
5. Boys to Men is a mentoring program one of our upper-level secondary education majors established. The program is for upper-level men at Carver to help mentor incoming freshman males in Carver, to create well-rounded and successful Black men. Each mentor has one to two mentees they support throughout the school year. Also, the Boys to Men group would do programming and outreach to Black boys in local schools. Allen was a mentee in the group.
6. A common Philadelphia slang term meaning *acting crazy or acting out of character*.
7. Critical Reading is one of the two reading remedial courses at Carver University.
8. Leon is referring to a workshop that another professor, Dr. Phillipe, and I ran to help students complete the application for the basic skills exam. The application is quite confusing and intimidating to some students, so the workshop was designed to walk students through the process step-by-step.

9. A magnet school is a public school commonly found in most urban school districts, where the often diverse and elite student population have to test into the school. Most magnet schools offer rigorous academic curricula.
10. This course is an upper-level sophomore class designed to teach math to elementary education majors. Tierra was misadvised and was not supposed to be taking this course her first semester of college.
11. Anything lower than 12 credits is considered part-time and financial aid does not support part-time students. Thus, if Tierra dropped the course, she would have had 11 credits and lost her funding.
12. The crediting body of collegiate sports, the NCAA, mandates that students need to be eligible to participate in a sport as long as their grades meet their standards.
13. Tierra, like other education majors at Carver University, wanted to major in special education. Most come to Carver assuming they have a special education major and then find out that they do not offer it, so they often end up majoring in elementary and/or early childhood education.
14. Jack & Jill is a strictly African American–based elite organization started in 1938. The organization plans social events for children between the ages of 2 and 19 (jackandjillinc.org).
15. Unfortunately, I never did figure out how to create a ringtone on my phone at that time.
16. City Year is a nonprofit program that works in public schools.
17. Center is the district's most prestigious magnet school.
18. SEPTA is the city's public transportation system.
19. Junior Year Practicum was a semester-long pre–student teaching experience.
20. Fundamentals is a nonprofit group in high school aimed at college preparation.
21. There is a large contingency of charter schools in Philadelphia, and many families need to apply ahead of time to have an alternative choice to their neighborhood school.
22. Promise Academies, at the time of this interview, were schools in the District of Philadelphia that were at more "risk" due to low test scores. Promise Academy schools often had longer teaching hours and the curriculum was set to have the students and schools accelerate their scores.
23. CP schools were schools in the District of Philadelphia that were reserved for youth kicked out of other neighborhood schools for severe disruptions or violence.
24. Transition week is the freshman orientation at Carver University.
25. A high school in a rural section of the state.
26. A K–8 school in a large urban area.
27. Unfortunately, midway through our dinner interview, the tape recorder stopped unbeknown to either of us. The rest of this section is Claresha's writing her thoughts on teaching.

REFERENCES

Akbar, R., & Sims, M. J. (2008). Surviving Katrina and keeping our eyes on the prize: The strength and legacy and tradition in New Orleans HBCU teacher preparation programs. *Urban Education, 43*(4), 445–462.

Albritton, T. J. (2012). Educating our own: The historical legacy of HBCUs and their relevance for educating a new generation of leaders. *Urban Review, 44*, 311–331.

Bennett, C. I., McWhorter, L. M., & Kuykendall, J. A. (2006). Will I ever teach? Latino and African American students' perspectives on Praxis I. *American Educational Research Journal, 43*, 531–575.

Boyer, J. B., & Baptiste, H. P. (1996). The crisis in teacher education in America: Issues of recruitment and retention of culturally different (minority) teachers. In J. Sikula (Ed.), *Handbook of research on teacher education* (2nd ed., pp. 779–794). New York: Simon and Schuster.

Carter, K., & Doyle, W. (1996). Personal narrative and life history in learning to teach. In J. Sikula (Ed.), *Handbook of research on teacher education* (2nd ed., pp. 120–142). New York: Macmillan Library Reference.

Clandinin, D. J. (1986). *Classroom practice: Teacher images in action.* Philadelphia: Falmer Press.

Costigan, A. (2004). Finding a name for what they want: A study of New York City's teaching fellows. *Teaching and Teacher Education, 20*, 129–143.

Dilworth, M. E. (2012). Historically Black Colleges and Universities in teacher education reform. *The Journal of Negro Education, 81*(2), 121–135.

Duhon-Sells, R. M., Peoples, V. A., Moore, W., & Page, A. T. (1996). Teacher preparation progams at historically Black colleges and universities. In J. Sikula (Ed.), *Handbook of research on teacher education* (2nd ed., pp. 779–794). New York: Simon and Schuster.

Etter-Lewis, G. (1996). From the inside out: Survival and continuity in African American women's oral narratives. In G. Etter-Lewis & M. Foster (Eds.), *Unrelated kin: Race and gender in women's personal narratives* (pp. 168–179). New York: Routledge.

Foster, M. (1996). Like us but not one of us: Reflections on a life history study of African American teachers. In G. Etter-Lewis & M. Foster (Eds.), *Unrelated kin: Race and gender in women's personal narratives* (pp. 215–228). New York: Routledge.

Foster, M. (1997). *Black teachers on teaching.* New York: New Press.

Gomez, M. L., Rodriguez, T. L., & Agosto, V. (2008). Life histories of Latino/a teacher candidates. *Teachers College Record, 110*(8), 1639–1676.

Gomez, M. L., & White, E. (2010). Seeing one another as "other." *Teaching and Teacher Education, 26,* 1015–1022.

Goodson, I., & Sikes, P. J. (2001). *Life history research in educational settings: Learning from lives.* Philadelphia: Open University Press.

Gordon, J. A. (2000). *The color of teaching.* London: RoutledgeFarmer.

Irvine, J. J., & Fenwick, L. T. (2011). Teachers and teaching for the new millennium: The role of HBCUs. *The Journal of Negro Education, 80*(3), 197–208.

Johnson, A. S. (2007). An ethics of access: Using life history to trace preservice teachers' initial viewpoints on teaching for equity. *Journal of Teacher Education, 58*(4), 299–314.

Johnson, S. M. (2007). *Finders and keepers: Helping new teachers survive and thrive in our schools.* San Francisco: Jossey-Bass.

Kelly, H. (2007). Racial tokenism in the school workplace: An exploratory study of Black teachers in overwhelmingly White schools. *Educational Studies, 41*(3), 230–254.

Lewis, C. (2006). African American male teachers in public schools: An examination of three urban school districts. *Teachers College Record, 108*(2), 224–245.

Lynn, M. (2002). Critical race theory and the perspectives of Black men teachers in the Los Angeles Public Schools. *Equity and Excellence in Education, 35*(2), 119–130.

Lynn, M. (2006). Education for the community: Exploring the culturally relevant practices of Black male teachers. *Teachers College Record, 108*(12), 2497–2522.

Milner, H. R., & Hoy, A. W. (2003). A case study of an African American teacher's self-efficacy, stereotype threat, and persistence. *Teaching and Teacher Education, 19*(2), 263–276.

Nettles, M. T., Scatton, L. H., Steinberg, J. H., & Tyler, L. L. (2011). Performance and passing rate differences of African American and White prospective teachers on Praxis examinations. *ETS Research Reports* 11–08. Retrieved from http://www.ets.org/Media/Research/pdf/RR-11-08.pdf

Petchauer, E. (2012). Teacher licensure exams and Black teacher candidates: Toward new theory and promising practice. *The Journal of Negro Education, 81*(3), 252–267.

Petchauer, E. (2013). Passing as White: Race, shame, and success in teacher licensure testing events for Black preservice teachers. *Race, Ethnicity, and Education.* DOI:10.1080/136133 24.2013.792796.

Rinke, C. (2009). Finding their way on: Career decision-making processes of urban science teachers. *Science Education, 93*(6), 1096–1121.

Roberts, M. A., & Irvine, J. J. (2009). African American teachers' caring behaviors: The difference makes a difference. In L. C. Tillman (Ed.), *The Sage handbook of African American education* (pp. 141–152). Los Angeles: Sage.

Simmons, C., Lewis, C., & Larson, J. (2011). Narrating identities: Schools as touchstones of endemic marginalization. *Anthropology & Education Quarterly, 42*(2), 121–133.

Sleeter, C. (2001). Preparing teachers for culturally diverse schools: Research and the overwhelming presences of whiteness. *Journal of Teacher Education, 52*(2), 94–106.

Su, Z. (1997). Teaching as a profession and as a career: Minority candidates' perspectives. *Teaching and Teacher Education, 13*(3), 325–340.

U.S. Bureau of Labor Statistics. (2008). *Labor force characteristics by race and ethnicity, 2008*. Washington, DC.

White House Initiative on Historically Black Colleges and Universities. (2013). What is an HBCU? Retrieved from http://www.ed.gov/edblogs/whhbcu/one-hundred-and-five-historically-black-colleges-and-universities/

ROCHELLE BROCK &
RICHARD GREGGORY JOHNSON III,
Executive Editors

Black Studies and Critical Thinking is an interdisciplinary series which examines the intellectual traditions of and cultural contributions made by people of African descent throughout the world. Whether it is in literature, art, music, science, or academics, these contributions are vast and far-reaching. As we work to stretch the boundaries of knowledge and understanding of issues critical to the Black experience, this series offers a unique opportunity to study the social, economic, and political forces that have shaped the historic experience of Black America, and that continue to determine our future. Black Studies and Critical Thinking is positioned at the forefront of research on the Black experience, and is the source for dynamic, innovative, and creative exploration of the most vital issues facing African Americans. The series invites contributions from all disciplines but is specially suited for cultural studies, anthropology, history, sociology, literature, art, and music.

Subjects of interest include (but are not limited to):

- EDUCATION
- SOCIOLOGY
- HISTORY
- MEDIA/COMMUNICATION
- RELIGION/THEOLOGY
- WOMEN'S STUDIES

- POLICY STUDIES
- ADVERTISING
- AFRICAN AMERICAN STUDIES
- POLITICAL SCIENCE
- LGBT STUDIES

For additional information about this series or for the submission of manuscripts, please contact Dr. Brock (Indiana University Northwest) at brock2@iun.edu or Dr. Johnson (University of San Francisco) at rgjohnsoniii@usfca.edu.

To order other books in this series, please contact our Customer Service Department:

(800) 770-LANG (within the U.S.)
(212) 647-7706 (outside the U.S.)
(212) 647-7707 FAX

Or browse online by series at www.peterlang.com.